The Knowledge

The Knowledge

The Power of Knowing How Life Works

Don Saunders

BALBOA.
PRESS

A DIVISION OF HAY HOUSE

ISBN: 978-1-4525-5388-7 (sc)
ISBN: 978-1-4525-5411-2 (hc)
ISBN: 978-1-4525-5387-0 (e)

Balboa Press books may be ordered through booksellers or by contacting:

Balboa Press
A Division of Hay House
1663 Liberty Drive
Bloomington, IN 47403
www.balboapress.com
1-(877) 407-4847

Because of the dynamic nature of the Internet, any web addresses or links contained in this book may have changed since publication and may no longer be valid. The views expressed in this work are solely those of the author and do not necessarily reflect the views of the publisher, and the publisher hereby disclaims any responsibility for them.

The author of this book does not dispense medical advice or prescribe the use of any technique as a form of treatment for physical, emotional, or medical problems without the advice of a physician, either directly or indirectly. The intent of the author is only to offer information of a general nature to help you in your quest for emotional and spiritual well-being. In the event you use any of the information in this book for yourself, which is your constitutional right, the author and the publisher assume no responsibility for your actions.

Any people depicted in stock imagery provided by Thinkstock are models, and such images are being used for illustrative purposes only.
Certain stock imagery © Thinkstock.

Printed in the United States of America

Library of Congress Control Number: 2012910966

Balboa Press rev. date: 6/22/2012

*This book is dedicated to my wife, Karen, and my sister, Sandy:
I love you both very much. Thank you for your total belief in me,
which has encouraged me to take the risks that lie ahead in
sharing this book with the world.*

*This book was inspired by my children, Jeff and Miranda,
who have always been a major joy in my life.*

Contents

Acknowledgements

The following people have contributed to my understanding of The Power of Knowing How Life Works each in their own way.

Thank you to my wife, Karen; my daughter, Miranda; my son Jeff; Brienna Prowler; Sandy and Bruce; all my family members; Michael and Jill; Joanne Shwed, editor, Author One Stop; Gilbert Prowler; Nikki Anderson; Loral Langemeier; Berny Dohrmann; Jill Lublin; Steve Lillo; Sara E. Smith; Holly Stamm; Howard Peters; Arne Ringstad; Valerie Malpass; Toni Pearce; John Radford; Mary Naasz; Bob Amos; JED Armstrong; Stuart Vreeburg; Todd Murdock; Monte Huff; Karol Whitlow; Dennis Mohl; Marty Estruch; Mike Toback; Dick Gilbert; Bob Cox; all my golf buddies in Vegas; the Olney neighbors; Andy Manna; David and Katy Stanley; Dr. David Gruder; my Mastermind teams and all of the members of CEO space; Steve and Aime McCrory at The Business Muse; the faculty and staff at The BEAM Institute a Learning Oasis @ Lake Las Vegas and my extended family in the Village @ Lake Las Vegas.

I would like to express a very special thank you, to two special people: Paul Hoyt a good friend and strategist and Randy Peyser at Author One Stop, Inc. both are exceptional professionals and should be considered by any author as an integral part of their writing and business process. The team took a project that was pushing the envelope in many directions and brought it back into focus for all of you to at least be able to ponder.

Thanks to all of you, and thanks to the universe for entrusting me with "The Knowledge"!

A Message from My Sister

Don, you are one beautiful, fantastic human being. I am overwhelmed by your new knowledge! I know your authenticity because I share your DNA. I have been privileged to walk this walk with you since Nov. 17, 2009. I know there is no way "The Knowledge" could have come to you other than the way you have experienced it. I watched you grow up; I know you. Your receipt of "The Knowledge" blows my mind, yet I believe you, unconditionally. Thanks for all you will be doing for the world. I know you are scared but the world needs this knowledge and it was delivered to you for a reason.

—Sandy

A taste: Our thoughts; feelings; beliefs; and emotions are not generated in our brains. They surround us and have been placed into the existing universal consciousness by people that have come before us for us to utilize.

The world is about to embark on an amazing journey!

The Box

Before you read this book, please do the following exercise:

1. Find a small box, such as a ring box with a lid, and come back to the book. (If you just want to humor me, and make an imaginary overture to pretend that you have a box in front of you, do that.)
2. Open the box.
3. Place in the box all of your traditional values, religious teachings and beliefs, political beliefs, and any prejudices you may have accumulated (not just racial prejudice but prejudice of all kinds, such as prejudice against tattoos, social differences, sexual orientation, relationship differences, and ethnic and religious prejudice).
4. Put the lid back on the box.
5. Do not leave the box behind at any time. Take it with you to eat, take it on breaks, and take it home. These are your values and your traditional beliefs, and no one—including yours truly—has the right to take any of those important thoughts from you at any time.

Now that you have safely put away your values and beliefs in the box, please **think out of the box** while *you are reading this book*. In fact, if at any time you feel I have taken you places you do not wish to go, open your box and take back whatever values or traditional thoughts you want, or need.

Your thoughts, feelings, beliefs and emotions, which you have stored safely in the box, belong to you; remember that is your past, not only your reality and your baggage but also your traditional learning's from years of programming.

"The Knowledge", which I received on Tuesday, Nov. 17, 2009, at 6:24 a.m., also belongs to you. I am merely the vehicle that the universe is using to deliver it. You remain in complete control. I am merely sharing knowledge, powerful as it may be it is still up to you to determine if it fits comfortably into your life.

Only you can determine what you would like to accept and what you would like to leave in the box. As you will discover, everything else goes back into the universe for someone else to utilize. It is how it all works.

Let us begin our amazing journey together! Thank you for caring enough about the future of humanity and equally important your future, to continue reading.

Foreword

I first met Don Saunders in a busy Las Vegas seminar room. Frankly, I didn't remember him when he reminded me of the time that he walked up to me, hugged me, and said, "I think you might be one of *them*!" He later explained that he knew I would somehow help him get his message out to the world. Don is very tenacious. He signed up right then and there for my next workshop and showed up a week later in San Diego. Don had a different agenda than most attendees who are looking for answers. Don *had* his answers; he just wasn't sure how to present and distribute them. It isn't possible for someone to simply have a quick discussion with Don in a hallway and expect a complete explanation. To understand the importance and depth of what came to him one November morning, you really need some background. That is why he wrote this book. In fact, he says he had no choice. *The Power of Knowing How Life Works* is a unique book. It's Don's true-life story about his goals, dreams, conquests, disappointments, and discouraging end to a long, corporate career.

Then his turnaround came: At 6:00 a.m. on Nov. 17, 2009, Don woke up to an experience that not only altered the course of his life but will possibly alter all of humanity's understanding of how our lives and the universe work—*forever*. In this book, Don reveals "The Knowledge" and insights that came to him during his remarkable journey beyond time and space. Imagine waking up to discover that you had just been presented with The Power of Knowing How Life Works!

Don reveals how "The Knowledge" he received provides a path to the solutions we all seek regarding the issues in our lives, and on the planet today, as he answers many of the biggest questions we ask ourselves, such as: *Why is life tough for some and easy for others? Which shapes us more – our destiny or our free will? What really happens when we die? How did the Universe begin and how does life function around us.*

Don emphasizes that he isn't a learned scholar, a highly educated philosopher, or a national celebrity; in fact, he refers to himself as "just an ordinary guy." Undoubtedly, he will have skeptics. Could this country boy from western New York State have attracted The Power of Knowing How Life Works? Don knows that "The Knowledge" was sent to him for everyone to analyze ... even *you*!

This is his experience and knowledge. He is not asking anyone to follow or worship him. He merely asks us to examine the possibility that the universe may be telling us something through various sources, and explains that he's only a vehicle to get "The Knowledge" out into the world. *What if he is?* Don has asked me not to commit any of my personal credibility into this foreword. He understands the volatility of discussing nontraditional facts without scientific confirmation. In good conscience, I cannot say that I understand the depth of "The Knowledge" that Don acquired during that minute in November 2009 because I didn't experience it. There is no proof, but I am going to suggest that you read on. At the very least, you will be intrigued at the possibilities he presents.

One thing I do know is that, when adversity hits or skeptics surface, he does not fold up and run away. Don feels compelled and determined to share "The Knowledge". He says that he's committed his life to dispense it to the world.

I encourage you to read the book. The worst case would be that you spent some time reading an interesting book; the best case would be that you ponder the question, "How does life as we know it work?"

Did Don get the answer and the corresponding insights delivered to him in those simple earthly minutes?

You decide!

Loral Langemeier
CEO of Live Out Loud, Inc.

Introduction

A True Story

While I am tempted to invite you to sit back, read, and enjoy this book, I think it would be better to advise you to sit on the edge of your seat as you devour every word and possibly gain a perspective that could help transform your life—*and possibly the world.*

It has been over two years since I started writing this book. It has also been over two years since I sat in my storage shed with a gun to my temple, wondering why all this crap we call "life" was happening to me. That was then; now I know why.

As I gain your confidence and build credibility with you, one thing is important to understand: What I am about to share is the truth—*my true-life experience*—and it is genuine and powerful. I manifested it very clearly without drugs, alcohol, or influence from any outside source other than the universe.

In the following pages, you will read about what led up to the actual experience on Nov. 17, 2009, at exactly 6:24 a.m., when I received a download of information (what I call "The Knowledge") that answered the "how" and the "why" questions as to how life really works. It was so extraordinary—and, in part, so unbelievable—that you might feel the urge to set this book aside many times and declare it science fiction.

It is not.

My Training

To be genuine in the distribution of "The Knowledge" I received, I realize in hindsight that I first needed to experience a giant smorgasbord of the ups and downs that life had to offer. I needed to live that life before my November experience in order to execute the insights and the answers to our biggest questions as to why we are here and what's it all about and how life works! I manifested these answers through a seemingly mystical source. I say "seemingly mystical" because while it may be mystical to you; to me, it was powerful and empowering reality.

After I was "fully trained" through living my life experiences (as you will come to read on the following pages), I was provided with "The Knowledge" to share with you ... and that's just the *beginning* of the story! I know how it happened. I know that I had a clear state of mind when it happened, and I know the result. I understand where I was, how I got there, and why I had the opportunity to experience the arrival of "The Knowledge".

When I was guided to write this book, I had no choice ... okay, yes I did. I could have ignored "The Knowledge", which, quite honestly, would have been the easy thing to do. I experienced very clear insights, which set me on the path of sharing "The Knowledge" with you. My insights provided me with the fact that "The Knowledge" is "on loan" to me; if I did not successfully figure out how to share this knowledge and, as importantly, all of the insights that came with it, I would lose all of it along the way. It would no longer surround me and would dissipate back into the universe. That is why I must distribute "The Knowledge"; I don't want to lose it – both for you and for me.

"The Knowledge" I am about to share with you is aimed at everyone on this planet. It didn't come from me; I was merely the vehicle through which it traveled. As you read, you may label the experience I had as a gift, a revelation, enlightenment, or knowledge. Regardless, your label does not change reality. It is a true story awaiting your analysis. The message I manifested on that extraordinary morning was more like one answer, complete with hundreds of corresponding insights. I was provided, The Power of Knowing How Life Works.

Just an Ordinary Guy

So, here are some things I want you to know about me as we start this journey together: I never thought there was anything unique about my life or about me. I spent 56 years walking the face of this earth in an average body, thinking I was "just an ordinary guy." I was a dedicated husband and father, a good provider, and a hard-working and fun-loving guy. I was very dedicated to my job and to the company that gave me an opportunity at an early age to earn a good living so I would not have to struggle in my later years.

I also coached baseball, basketball, and soccer for 11 years while my children were growing up. Two kids who played baseball with us even went to the pros. I remember dealing with a few of the players' family issues, including depression, fear, and other conflicts at home and at school. While coaching, I laid some good foundations for these young athletes, but now I know that everything I did was all part of my training for what was to come.

The Purpose of This Book

In just a few moments I am going to tell you about the set of overwhelming circumstances that led to the enormous "data dump" of empowering knowledge that I experienced on November 17, 2009. This "data dump" was almost too unbelievable for me to comprehend … *and I was there!* At every juncture, I applied a critical "litmus test," as I reviewed the content you are about to read regarding my experience in each of the following chapters. I asked myself, "So what? Why will people care about what I have to tell them?"

Outside of the intrigue or curiosity that you may have about what happened to me as I received "The Knowledge" in this inconceivable data dump, I believe the biggest reason you will care about what I have to share with you is that "The Knowledge" will help you to sort out the "why" questions of your life. It will give you simple answers about how "it" all works, even if you:

- Feel that you are already enlightened but may have some gaps in your knowledge; this information will fill those gaps.
- Think that you have all the answers you need in order to be satisfied;
- Compare your theories with those of "The Knowledge"; or
- Turn your head, throw up your arms, or cup your hands over your ears because you just don't want to know or don't believe that someone has received "The Knowledge" after hundreds of years of civilization.

It took me 47 years to prepare for the receipt of "The Knowledge", since I had been asking the question, *How does life work?*, since I was 10 years old. I had no prior understanding about how life worked. I now realize that not having had anyone to explain to me anything about the workings of the universe had made me a perfect candidate to receive "The Knowledge" because I was sheltered from any outside influences that would have made me question, judge or dismiss what I'd experienced on that morning in November 2009.

From the positive responses I have received from those who have heard my experience, I am almost certain that the majority of people who are finding their way to my message would appreciate a shortcut to understanding "The Knowledge", and that is my purpose for writing this book. .

"The Knowledge" has been delivered to me because I have been trained to deliver it to you. *It was delivered for you.* I will not tell you how to live your life—plenty of people try to do that already—but I will instead share with you how I fixed mine.

I hope that telling you my story will allow me to live in peace with "The Knowledge". (I am probably not going to have much peace when this book hits the news because of the potential controversy it might stir up, but it was a nice thought!)

Why Me?

I never imagined that I would have answers to the world's major problems, let alone "The Knowledge" about how life really works. However, now that "The Knowledge" has settled in, I fully realize that I was in training my entire life to be receptive to it when it arrived.

Prior to this experience, I had no idea that there was an "existing" consciousness community already producing books, DVDs, videos, and seminars to make and "identify" a conscious change in the world regarding how we look at life, such as *The Secret* and *Tapping the Source*.

When my "data download" happened, the information I received was all new, fresh, and powerful to me. But as I started to meet people from the consciousness community, I was confused as to why the universe had sent me "The Knowledge" since it appeared to me that others already understood how it all worked. Early in the process, when I first shared my experience with Loral Langemeier (my then mentor and personal coach), she said, without fully understanding or listening, "Don, we *know* that already!"

This made me question: Why download "The Knowledge" to me—a country boy and just an ordinary guy—if the consciousness community was already at work with this information? Why did the universe send *me* "The Knowledge"? Why am I different from all of the other motivational and inspirational self-help authors? What makes me think (or know!) that I can touch three hundred million people in America and then seven billion people in the world?

Because it's painfully obvious that the world is still floundering after all of the writings and the movies, the newfound religions, the traditional religions and worthy causes that have dotted the globe. I've never heard any other people say that they actually manifested "The Knowledge" from as far back as the beginning of time. I was provided with insights that will help individuals sustain healthy, joyous, and prosperous lives, and with Knowledge that can provide the power to sustain society for billions of years to come. If people will only take time to listen and then actually ponder the possibilities.

The Power of Knowing How Life Works is not "my" theory or belief. It contains the truth about how life works. "The Knowledge" gives real-life answers to those who have not yet figured out how to help themselves. It has the potential to help millions understand the simplest as well as the most complex issues of life.

I know what the answer is as to how life really works, but it's *my answer*. I will share it, but I will not ask anyone to agree with me. I will only ask of you that you *listen with an open intent to learn*. "The Knowledge", which surrounds you, will provide the answers if you listen. In the end, it really does not matter what you label the source. The execution of "The Knowledge" as to how you can lead a better and happier life is really what counts. The source as you will see is the same for all of us. Our labels are different.

Although I can't deny what happened, I am not "a chosen one" (as one guy tried to call me in a valiant effort to assign a label). I hold no mystical powers. I have no illusions about my sudden answers and insights. I have not experienced "born again" religious phenomena. I can't foresee the future. I am not a psychic or a medium. I saw no white lights or bolts of lightning. I am not a mystic, shaman or guru of any kind.

I cannot state this any more clearly: *I am just an ordinary guy*. However, I was able to recognize the insights and answer that arrived as "my own." I have never been an avid reader or watched many documentaries on television. And as I mentioned, I wasn't interested in anything much more than work, family, friends, golf, and maybe a little poker along the way. So, it was clear to me that the experience of receiving the insights and the answer to all the "why" questions of how life works was pure and genuine and not a recollection of things I may have read or watched.

What I'm about to share was not delivered with a religious foundation, nor is this a politically motivated book. I am not searching for followers or a congregation. I am sharing the information—nonpolitical, multi-denominational or nondenominational, and non-prejudicial—as it was delivered to me. There is no hidden agenda, no cult, no new religion, no new political party, and no prejudicial exclusion.

- I will never run for political office or form a new political party
- I will never start what appears to be a church-based religious order.
- I will never ask anyone to follow me to utopia under false claims.

At first, I used the term "gift" to describe "The Knowledge", but my advisors—okay, my wife and kids!—did not like the inference of that word because it sounded as though I had a religious awakening and God had chosen me to spread "the Word." I believe that some will "get it"; a few will say, "We knew that"; others will say, "Sure, whatever"; still others may say I have "seen the light" and God has chosen me to do His work. Maybe some will tell me that I have been "born again" or something along those lines.

Was God talking to me? That can be left to interpretation. As I've mentioned, "The Knowledge" was delivered to me with no return address or label on the information. It was just a special-delivery download of knowledge. *Most importantly, "The Knowledge" was meant to fit into everyone's belief system.* My story is a true story that will, at the very least, make you ponder the possibilities and generate some of your own questions about how life works.

The way I see it, I am just an ordinary guy with "an impossible task": to distribute "The Knowledge", which was delivered directly to me from the universe with no third-party intermediary step to misinterpret it. The fun part is that I know it is available to all of you through the same channel.

"The Knowledge" is powerful, and the delivery vehicle (me) remains humble and honored to have received "The Knowledge". I have been trained to deliver "The Knowledge" and will document with words and confirm with actions that "The Knowledge" is pure, and the only intent is to deliver it and nothing else—no riots, no protest, no violence, and no uprisings of any kind.

Many people will challenge "The Knowledge" and they have the right to do so. I go to sleep every night with the confidence that "The Knowledge" is genuine and pure. Can you say the same about all of your traditional teachings? Just suppose I really did get "The Knowledge" delivered directly from the universe! Then, consider that the reason "The Knowledge" was delivered to me was that we have gone far enough off the path and need a major correction. Not led by politicians or religious leaders but simply just an ordinary guy that has been provided extraordinary knowledge.

I Manifested the Download

I had no doubt why "The Knowledge" came to me; with the passing of every day, it gets clearer. I manifested "The Knowledge" from the universe since I was 10 years old. It took 47 years, but it arrived in a very clear, vivid delivery. "The Knowledge" was already in the universe so, as I manifested the download, it was readily available. Forty-seven years is a blink of an eye in comparison to the development of the universe. So technically in universal terms I probably received "The Knowledge" almost as soon as I asked for it.

I was clearly shown the beginning of the universe because the world needs to understand how it all started in a pure explanation and not with scientific theory. Why do I have the audacity to believe that I have "The Knowledge" of how the universe began? *Because I do!*

It is not opinion or theory; it is fact. However, before all of the skeptics start down the paths of trying to disprove "The Knowledge", let me remind everyone that it is *my knowledge and my knowledge only.* I am willing to share it because that is why it was delivered to me.

You do not have to believe it. You do not have to accept it. You are free to keep your traditional beliefs and I will respect you for doing so. In fact, I believe that others have had "The Knowledge" delivered to them, but the world would not listen, the individual did not know how to deliver it, they became afraid, or they just quit trying.

Why Should I Bother?

When I explain the full picture of how life works, you will start to understand why we know as much as we know and how knowledge comes to us. Many insights will seem familiar, many have been taught for centuries, and many are so basic that I could have discounted "The Knowledge" as something that everybody already knew.

So why should I bother telling anyone?

The strength of "The Knowledge" was so overwhelming, and the power of the energy (for lack of a better earthly word) was so powerful, I could not discount it. I could not set it aside as something that we already had. It arrived in such a pure form that I knew there was a deeper meaning to each insight other than what I was seeing on the surface.

You Do Not Know What You Do Not Know

History has resulted in some wrong conclusions about how life works. Until now, it has been "you do not know what you do not know."

The Power of Knowing How Life Works will answer these long, sought-after questions:

- How did the universe begin?
- How does life, as a physical being, work?
- What happens when we die?
- How do we take control of our lives and claim our paths going forward?

If you believe that you already know these things, please help distribute the collective universal knowledge. When you plant the answer and insights into the universal knowledge base and watch it take root, your life and the lives of others will start to produce positive results.

There are seven billion people throughout the world, including more than three hundred million Americans, who could learn something from "The Knowledge" and the corresponding insights, if they choose to do so. By keeping an open mind to the potential, consider the possibility that we may never have had the real answers or necessary tools to understand how life works—from beginning to end and back again.

I am not egotistical enough to believe that I am the only recipient of "The Knowledge" over the centuries. There have been many but our universal knowledge base had not advanced enough to give us a basis for the truth.. Offering "The Knowledge", with its powerful content, still presents an interesting task of how to distribute it. Then, to have people accept it as the empowering revolutionary knowledge that it is, presents a challenge. I have no choice but to accept the challenge.

The world is complex, and part of my insights has shown me to be patient. As I have learned recently from reading about the ancient Toltec civilization; I don't take things personally and make no assumptions.

You Have the Power

I hope that, as you read this book, you will start to understand that you have the power to manifest your own answers and insights in life. Perhaps, if you read carefully, I can provide you with some sort of shortcut. It took me 56 years to find the answer and I'm happy to share it with you.

"The Power of Knowing How Life Works" has affected my existence. It has arrived, and now as I share it, it is up to you to figure out what to do with this information. One thing I do know is that as you come to understand ""The Knowledge"," and share it with others, we will create a better world.

Most of the world walks around in neutral mode, now for purposes of this book and the explanation of ""The Knowledge"" neutral mode is not intended to be bad. If you are in neutral mode it simply means that you get up in the morning, put your feet on the floor, go do what you normally do all day, come home, have some dinner, watch some TV or maybe sit at your computer and then go to bed. If you enjoy statistics that is about 98% of the population. You have 1% of the population that considers themselves part of the consciousness community and of course the 1% of the elite greed and profit class.

It is time for you to TAKE BACK YOUR PERSONAL POWER using ""The Knowledge""

My Experience

When and Where It All Started

I was born in 1953 in western New York to a mother in her 40s, who made some positive declarations about my future; she declared that I was born to change the world. Now, that in itself is no surprise. Every mother wants her child to be successful, so maybe it meant nothing; unfortunately, she is no longer around to ask.

At the age of 10, standing on a pile of freshly mowed hay, I decided that I did not want to spend my life working on a farm. Not that there is anything wrong with that. It doesn't take a farm boy long to realize that farm work is hard and is never going to get any easier. I knew then that I wanted to work at a job where I wore a tie and a nice shirt. The place to do that was in the largest city closest to my hometown; Rochester, New York. I knew that I was going to get a job there with a big company. I knew that I was going to be somebody and do something with my life.

I stated my life's vision aloud to all the other guys: "I am going to go to work for the largest company in western New York."

At age 10, I had lots of time to grow up and, at that point, I didn't know what a powerful statement I was making. Nevertheless, I went about my life and knew that no one was going to stop me from success.

I had set my course.

Lying under the Country Stars

As far back as I can remember (somewhere around the age of 8 or 10, and continuing until I left home at around 17 or 18), I spent the majority of my summer evenings—sometimes with my friends but mostly by myself—doing what the cowboys did: I slept under the stars. The houses back then had no air conditioning so, if your bedroom was at the top of the house with no air circulation or fan, the heat was stifling on those hot, humid summer nights.

On those warm summer evenings, I had no tent, just a blanket spread out over the ground. I would lie back, looking up at the stars, the moon, and the beautiful country sky, which overlooked western New York. On a clear evening, you could see nearly every star in the sky. Country skies are illuminating and powerful; there are no city lights to contaminate the brilliance from the stars. I tried counting the stars, but that became a futile effort. I also watched many other unique objects in the universe. Those nights provided some of the most peaceful, calming moments of my life.

On those nights, the universe belonged only to me—or at least it felt that way. As I lay there, I proclaimed my plans and stored them in my mind. There was no way I could have understood any of the theories, philosophies, or scientific explanations that pertained to how life works. I was a poor country kid, never exposed to that kind of thinking. I was doing what I now understand as manifesting my future and asking pertinent questions that actually would lead to "The Knowledge" being delivered with amazing details and clarity.

"How Does This All Work?"

As I looked up at the evening sky, I always asked, "How does this all work?" Some of you may have asked that same question once or maybe numerous times in your life; however, I asked it every day of my life—*every day.*

I don't remember expressing this question to any specific source; in other words, I never asked, "God, how does this all work?" I simply asked the beautiful country sky. I never expected any kind of answer, but it seemed like a fair question to ponder when no one else was listening (at least I *thought* no one was listening).

A Vision Before I Met My Wife

Something quite remarkable took place the day my best friend Mike and I were driving around town. As we passed a white house, I looked at Mike and he looked back at me. It felt as if time had stood still.

"I'm going to marry the girl who lives in that house!"

Without hesitation, and still looking in my eyes, he said, "I know! *I know!*"

That experience may not be so strange in most cases, except for the fact that I truly did not know if a girl even lived in that house, let alone someone I knew.

Later, I asked Mike if he remembered what had happened.

"I *think* I remember something like that, but I don't really even remember driving down to the village that day." (Actually, we both knew that he had because his younger brother's friend told on Mike and, of course, his brother then passed that information along to his Dad.) We were then back to walking for a while as the car sat in the garage.

I later realized that I had experienced what Native Americans spend hours in sweat lodges trying to attract: a "vision." I have never had another one since then, but I know it was a vision.

How do I know with all my heart and soul that I had a vision? Well, one chilly Saturday, when I was a junior in high school, we had a football game. After the game, this girl (the captain of the cheerleading team) and I (the captain of the football team) were at an after-game party. She had a fight with her boyfriend and I offered to walk her home—*right up to that white house.* I did not tell her then, but I knew that I had just walked my wife home for the first time. At the time of this writing we have been happily married 39 years.

Terrible Accidents

At the age of 16 or 17, I lost seven good friends, including Mike, all in separate incidents. We lived in a very small, rural town with graduating classes of around 50, so losing seven friends was tough for many of us. When this happened, I started including these events into my daily question of "How does this all work?"

I held daily conversations with each of these seven deceased friends my entire life. They were one sided conversations of course but they took place none the less. I asked them if they had the ability to send back some input please feel free to do so. I still had no expectation of ever receiving any answers. Now of course I realize; that is not how it works.

Choosing the Fork in My Road

My parents had worked hard to build a public campground out of our 50-acre hay field. Dad said he built it for me; the reality was that he did it for himself. However, now that I was 18 and finishing high school, and was old enough to start the process of taking over the business, he wanted me to stick around and help run things.

He made no demands about it, but it was obvious that he wanted me to keep his work alive. He used subtle comments like, "I have no money to send you to college" and "Why go to college when you have a business already in place for you?" *Ouch!*

Those environmental roadblocks are typically present in your daily life, as if someone were grabbing you by the collar from behind and pulling you backward.

I chose to go to college. At around the same time, I was a drummer with enough talent to become a professional musician. I was dating my wife and, instead of staying with the music, I chose to focus on a steady job and paycheck.

I decided to get my business degree, go to work in corporate America, and raise a family. I also continued to play drums on weekends for extra cash and, in my later years, was a member of a rock and roll band, which once opened for the Beach Boys while my son was attending West Virginia University. (Hey, we all need our 30 minutes of fame!)

I graduated from the first two years of college with an associate degree. I then went to work as a summer employee at the same company I had envisioned at age 10! They hired me full time and offered to pay for the rest of my education if I would go to school in the evenings and work for them during the day. I was able to finish my four-year degree by going nights and weekends. This accomplishment was another powerful manifestation from my childhood as I was the first of eight children to receive my college degree. I had set obtaining a degree as a goal for most of my youth—another great training exercise.

I continuously planned and plotted my future, which I had unknowingly manifested into my reality. For a country boy with no money, the offer of a full-time job at this company was like hitting the lotto.

I worked in the basement of the company, putting together notebooks for their sales training courses. I eventually worked my way up the ladder as the youngest sales rep they had ever sent out into the field. I was 21 years old and we were on our way to California. Leaving our families behind was very tough on my wife and me, but we were young and accepted the cross-country assignment.

Visualizing "Out Loud"

I can clearly remember an instance where I visualized my intentions "out loud." I was a rookie salesman, standing on a tee box at a golf resort in Scottsdale, Arizona.

I looked at my regional manager and said, "Someday, I want to be a regional manager, just like you. I want to live in a beautiful golf resort, just like this. And I want to have a beautiful house on the golf course, just like that one." I pointed to a small house along the course.

My boss laughed. "You can have *all* that. Just stay focused and work hard."

These days, I am sure that many country kids are exposed to golf and the ways of the world more than I was. However, if you grew up as a city kid, you cannot possibly understand how living in rural America kept you pure of thought and isolated. I grew up in the country where golf was never mentioned. We had no idea what drugs were, and we saw hundreds of acres of farm crops instead of golf courses.

The American Dream

From that point on, I was living the American dream. I always had a decent home and earned a good living, which allowed me to support my family. I had a great job, a nice car, and the potential for a lucrative retirement if I worked hard and stayed focused. I had two great kids and a spectacular wife with which to share it.

The company moved us six times—always to clean up a failing sales territory—but also rewarding me with more pay or an impressive title. I mentored new salespeople and eventually ended up as a vice president of sales for the western United States for one division of the company. During those moves—six cities, thousands of new people, and just as many perspectives on life—I learned about the diversity across America.

A Good Plan Gone Awry

It was a good master plan—right up until I was 54 years and four months old. When the company, to which I had dedicated my life for more than 35 years, decided that they were going to sell off my division eight months short of my 55th birthday, it meant that I was not going to be able to retire as planned. You had to be 55 for the formulas to kick in.

I would be losing a significant portion of my retirement annuity and all of my health and dental benefits. This was a simple case of posttraumatic job disorder—not funny for people who are suffering from it. It is deadly serious and needs to be carefully examined.

Even though the company had smacked me down hard, the management of that company felt that everything would be okay because we were all offered jobs in the new company, which had bought us out. They could sleep soundly at night thinking that they had done us all a favor. They could not have been more wrong in their assumptions. As part of the transition they made it very clear that we would be starting from square one, with no pension plans and no significant income at the end of the rainbow. We were up the proverbial creek without a paddle. Because they laid out the plan with lots of big, corporate lawyers, we had no legal recourse. I might add that the CEO kept his retirement and benefits in tact along with significant bonuses for carrying out the sale.

What about Retirement?

I was an older worker with no visible means of support. I couldn't retire, even though I knew it was what they were trying to force me to do, because I had no retirement income to allow me to make that choice. When my company discovered that it wasn't going to be as easy as sending me a signal that they wanted me to leave, they downsized my area of responsibility and set me up to fail.

At 54, I had achieved my vision from age 20. I was living in a beautiful golf resort in Nevada. (Please note that, after living in the resort for two years, I discovered that the developer was the same one who had built the Arizona resort where I had stood on the tee box with my new boss and proclaimed my "out loud" intentions some 30 years earlier!)

Without a significant retirement income, I had set myself in a position that I could not sustain. An additional and stressful problem was that the older guys in the company—all my good friends—no longer had the security of the "golden parachutes," so we had to hang on for our lives because we had no choice— at least that's how we felt.

Because I was close to retirement, living in a golf resort, and "assuming" that I had enough money in my retirement plan to give me a good life, I stopped visualizing my future because I thought I had reached my goals. I found myself in neutral mode.

I went into a very deep, life-threatening depression. I eventually left on my own accord because the corporate life was destroying me, piece by piece.

The Storage Shed

I was fighting major depression over several things in my life: I lost my retirement income from a company sell-out, and my home property values devalued. Additionally, my company now (incorrectly) believed that I was too old to be a salesperson, I didn't have the GQ look they thought I should have; consumers' buying attitudes had plunged and my wife's retail outlet products were not selling due to an economic slump. All in all, my long-range future seemed quite bleak.

Feeling these stresses and worries, one day I headed for the shed where I stored my guns. I unboxed the guns and set them by my side. I sat there for what could have been an hour or so, rationalizing the pros and cons and trying to justify my contemplated actions: My insurance would provide my wife of 37 years the security that I could not seemingly provide for her.

I sat in the shed and held the not-yet-loaded gun to my head. Then, I had a major flash of reality: Would the insurance pay off on suicide? With that nagging question bearing down on me, I set the gun down and decided that I would check the insurance policy.

When I arrived back home to check the policy, my wife knew that something was seriously wrong. She forced me to tell her the story of my experience at the storage shed. Her reaction was not what you might have expected; in fact, it caught me totally off guard.

Instead of the hug and tears (which, of course, followed closely behind), she lashed out with the following yell:

"How *dare* you think that our 37-year relationship was about money! How *dare* you think that an insurance check is the answer to my future!"

I have lived on all points of the sliding scale we call "life," but I had never felt the level of despair that led up to that moment. Until you walk in someone's shoes, you can "care" but you can never really understand. I am now able to understand those in despair.

The Power of Tears

I was experiencing debilitating, life-threatening stress. I felt the intense physical gripping pain in my body that wouldn't let up. I found it hard to move, let alone breathe. I had constant headaches and was depressed every day. At the encouragement of my wife and doctor, and after disclosing the experience of sitting in the storage shed with a gun, I agreed to meet with a therapist for a couple of visits.

At the first session, the power of tears (unheard of for me because I am a macho, tough country kid!) allowed me to release an incredible buildup of emotional pain. I talked about issues that brought me to the "couch" in the first place.

On the way to my reluctant second meeting with the therapist—Monday, Nov. 16, 2009—I vowed that I would pull myself together and not have a similar, tearful meltdown during this session as I had the first time. When I got to her office, I proceeded to "the safe room," as she called it. The pep talk I gave to myself on the drive over didn't work.

The tears started again and I was more than a bit embarrassed. (After all, I am a man, and men "suck it up.") Although my therapist assured me at the first session that the release of tears was therapeutic and gave me "permission" to stop crying, with the second session, I brought tears to *her* eyes with my stories.

I shared the pain, which had lingered unspoken for almost 40 years, of losing seven friends in high school. I told her how the draft lottery placed me at 361 out of 365, so I did not have to go to Viet Nam. I admitted my lifelong guilt for not serving my country and, for a country kid, how that duty to my country was important to me. I also explained that I constantly wondered, "Why them and not me?" Why did I not end up in Viet Nam? (One of my friends had died of Agent Orange exposure.)

I wanted to know how this all worked but, of course, she could not tell me. Instead, she helped me realize that I had learned to "cope" with my unresolved feelings by never sharing that grief with anyone. With her help, I started to cope with my stress and depression.

My Homework Assignment

As I got up from the couch at the end of the hour-long session, she said, "Hang on! You have a homework assignment."

"Okay," I thought, "why not?"

She asked me if I had ever heard of the book entitled *The Secret* by Rhonda Byrne.

"No," I responded. "Actually, I have never taken time in my life for leisure reading of any kind because, every time I tried, I would nod off. In fact, I have never read a book in its entirety, even though I have a four-year college degree."

(I now understand that, although it may be perplexing and sound contrite, the universe did not want me to read books. If I had been a reader, someone else's beliefs, theories, or guesses would have influenced me as to how life worked. The universe deliberately kept me from reading so, when "The Knowledge" was provided, there would be absolutely no doubt in my mind as to its origin. I would accept "The Knowledge" as pure and genuine from the source.)

Nevertheless, I promised my therapist that I would buy *The Secret,* although, in the back of my mind, I knew I would not read it. I bought the book, took it home, set it neatly next to my television chair (where all books start out before they end up unread on the shelf), and left it on the table to read some other time (maybe, but probably not).

The Event

The next day, on Tuesday, Nov. 17, 2009, I awoke at exactly 6:00 a.m. I know this because I looked at the digital clock at the foot of our bed—and something terrifying and unexpected was happening to me. I was paralyzed from the neck down.

I saw the clock, and acknowledged that it was there, but when I tried to step out of bed to do my morning exercise routine, I could not move. I could not reach over to wake up my wife and, until I figured out what might be happening, I did not want to yell out and frighten her. Looking back, I'm not even sure if I could have yelled. All I could do was lie on my back and watch the clock tick off minutes. As it did, tears began to flow from my eyes. I had no idea what was happening to me. Panic thoughts raced through my mind.

"Is my life over? Is that all there is to it?"

The clock ticked for what seemed like an eternity. I felt as if I had slept for 100 years but I was awake the entire time and watched the minutes pass. I was calm as the clock remained on 6:23. My traditional thoughts, beliefs, and history drained from around me, and I put my traditional values in my box. I cleared the hard drive.

When the clock ticked 6:24 a.m., the download began. I was locked into one minute of earth time, but it represented billions of years of universal experiences. My paralysis enabled me to receive the entire download and complete the entire process.

Then, an event occurred that can only be compared to watching a tornado. Explosive images, running like a fast 3D movie in the background, and scenes from the Great Depression and the Dust Bowl era, flooded my mind. It was like Dorothy in the *Wizard of Oz* when she and her little dog, Toto, were being blown in circles through the sky as she watched her life pass through the window of her house.

Women were screaming, babies were crying, and people were fighting over materialistic and idealistic things. Images of Dr. Martin Luther King, Jr., and President John F. Kennedy flashed through my head at nanosecond speed; pictures of Bill Gates, Warren Buffett, Oprah Winfrey, Dr. Phil McGraw, Ellen DeGeneres, and Rachel Ray, mixed in with hundreds of other images of people I couldn't identify, all raced by. (I have never met any of these people.) I know now, without hesitation, that their presence was significant or will be at some future point in my life.

In a flash, I saw myself in front of a large audience with thousands of people listening to me. I did not know what it all meant, but later, when I turned on the television and saw Joel Osteen talking, tears came to my eyes. I had seen the same setting (minus Joel) and I was the person in front of the crowd.

The clock was still at 6:24. I was awake, paralyzed, and unable to move. My mind was clear and empty, and my problems and stress had dissipated. I was now processing 1000's of insights and affirming "The Knowledge" that had arrived.

Clear Space

I visualized a place with no significant surroundings. Nothing—and I mean *nothing*—was visible for a portion of the experience. Empty space eventually turned into outlines of clear dots and clear waves. Then, as these items came into focus, they evolved into floating white dots and waves of multiple colors.

I ended up in a "clear space"—a space that I have not been able to duplicate in real time. When I say "clear," I mean it had no color, no boundaries, no definition, no reflection, and no darkness or brightness. There was no beginning and no end; in other words, it was infinite. It was the beginning of the universe.

The clear space had no solid matter, no atoms, no molecules, no cells, just empty space. While I was trying to determine where I was and what I was looking at, during what could have been billions of years of universal time but less than one minute of earth time, I was provided knowledge of some incredible things.

The understanding of this is not easy because describing "clear" in this context is impossible. It means that there is no visual existence of anything. It is pure clear. Also, to claim that something is "infinite" is wrong because that word has a specific definition in the dictionary (i.e., "extending indefinitely") and "clear" and "infinite" to which I am referring, is undefined.

Dots and Waves

Developing before my eyes were clear dots and waves— what may be described in traditional lay terms as something you might see over a long stretch of paved road on a brutally hot summer day. We simply call it "heat," but it is visual "energy" (again, for lack of a better earthly word). Earthly words that keep us from measuring something new have confused our focus.

Eventually, the waves—but, more noticeably, the dots—had substance to them; many were coming into focus in a white format. I'd rather not call the forming of the universe "energy" because energy is a man-made word. The timeframe I am talking about was before any life, so that words cannot apply. Actually, no words can apply to any of what I am telling you for the same reason. They exist but we have yet to discover it.

From that clear space, which I have the knowledge of, the phenomena (or "particles," for lack of a better word) were attracted to each other and formed solid matter. The corresponding knowledge was confirming the process as it happened.

"The Knowledge" clarified that the phenomenon appeared in two forms: dots and waves. As the dots attracted together to form solids, which eventually ended up as planets and stars, the waves held everything in place. It is also possible that, before I could understand anything I was able to comprehend, such as the waves and dots, there could have been a gaseous state but that was not indicated in "The Knowledge". I pose that potential only as a possibility, so scientists do not discount the option of the existence of a gas in their pursuit of the beginning components contained in the clear space.

After the Event

When the clock ticked 6:25 a.m., it was over. I could feel sensation and life returning to my body. Insights were in my mind, which had not been there before. Something incredible had just happened and everything felt fresh and new.

According to the clock, it was only one minute and it ended as suddenly as it had begun … *or had it?* I was somewhere for a very long time based on the amount of information I acquired … *or was I?*

I jumped out of bed, grabbed a piece of paper, and wrote my still-sleeping wife a note: "I went to exercise. Love you. *I might have it!*" (She still has the note.) I did not know or completely understand what had happened to me, but I knew it was big!

When I got to the gym, I felt like a 30-year-old. I ripped through my routine with ease. As I paced away on the elliptical machine, I closed my eyes and tears flowed down my face as I reflected on what had just taken place. Ninety minutes passed in what seemed like an instant.

The next morning, I was sitting in my television chair, typing away. I needed to capture this remarkable experience in writing. For days—without clearly understanding where it was coming from or where it was going to take me—endless thoughts and images traveled through what I now refer to as my processor and they also surrounded me. I was frantic and felt compelled to write everything down.

Page after page, the words poured out at an incredible pace. I wrote on just about anything I could get my hands on—paper, napkins, and the computer. I had to get every word, every inference, and every insight down in writing.

In two days, nearly 80,000 words rolled from my fingers to the paper and keyboard. The writing was a way for me to deal with and work it all out. I was not frightened, overwhelmed, psychotic, or unrealistic. I ate, slept, and interacted with my family. I was simply entranced and mesmerized by the information springing into my life. It was as if a bomb had gone off next to me and I was shell-shocked.

New Insights

My experience took place while I was awake; this was not a dream. Well over a year after my November 2009 experience, I was still afraid to speak about it to others. I knew that sharing the information haphazardly or relentlessly with those who had no time to digest it or had no interest in it, would not make me a good steward of "The Knowledge".

After the event, my sister and wife both reminded me of an instance, approximately 30 years ago, when I woke up paralyzed. I specifically remember forcing myself onto the floor with a great deal of effort because I was scared. Some weird feelings surrounded me back then, but I had disrupted whatever was taking place. I had a complete physical and the doctors found nothing. I have now concluded that I was either not ready or I disrupted the download at that point and continued to live my life.

As I started speaking about my experience, some commented, "Don, I follow you right up to the point where you state you were temporarily paralyzed. That sounds a little contrived." I now know that my paralysis left me no choice but to accept the download of "The Knowledge" from the universe. I could not shake it off or disrupt it with a sudden pounce out of bed. In talking to people, it has become apparent that they "hear" the explanation of what happened but are not able to grasp the enormity of the experience.

I also know that I could have been streaming thoughts from the universe for hours, probably years in universal time, all as the clock remained locked on 6:24, as my body lay paralyzed based on the massive amount of information that now surrounds me. I was at the beginning of the universe, with knowledge of how time began. It was not the same as when people describe out-of-body experiences. It was exclusive to the surrounding area of my body, not leaving any one point but merely obtaining knowledge and information as it surrounded to me.

Another important observation was the total absence of anything related to science fiction in my life. I had no interest in sci-fi, including movies, books, or conversations. I was always confused as to why everyone loved it and why I was immune to it all. I never watched a *Star Trek* movie and always made excuses to be doing something else when kids my age, as well as my own kids, went to the movie theater to see anything in this genre. I know now that it prevented me from disregarding the information, which I received that November morning, as a rewind of somebody else's imagination.

The Beginning of the Universe and Science

Clear Space and Zero-point Fields

As we know the beginning of the universe started billions of years ago, fueled by a phenomenon not yet discovered. For purposes of this book the existing theories of energy or a superior being can remain intact, but we must have missed some fine points; otherwise, I would not have been given the powerful information to share with you.

For example, scientists have already investigated zero-point fields. To explain a bit, in quantum field theory, the "vacuum state" (also called the "vacuum") is the quantum state with the lowest possible energy. Generally, it is believed to contain no physical particles. The term "zero-point field" is synonym for the vacuum state of an individual quantized field. In simple terms, it is a point where *nothing* exists. The very beginning of the universe was in this state. Or was it? "The Knowledge" challenged the vacuum state. There is something we missed that is no longer a secret.

To the best of my knowledge, scientists understand and acknowledge the existence of zero-point fields, but I have not found documentation where a scientist has proclaimed that the zero-point field was the beginning of the universe. They know they are close, but there is still a missing element. It is an unknown and unmeasured phenomenon, which we have mistakenly labeled many times as "energy."

For lack of a better explanation, we have assigned the word "creation" to the concept of a "superior being." I am not trying to change your spiritual beliefs; in fact, if society would accept some weird, unknown word that I made up, I could then label the beginning of the universe something else because it is clear that it is a source unknown to science or traditional thought. It is the missing piece of the puzzle.

We do not have it correct just yet, but I was given no mathematical formula or scientific theory to explain it to you—and I know why. "The Knowledge" of how the universe began is already available in the universe. It is up to people much more focused on science and discovery than I am to manifest the technical analysis of information and prove the science.

As I mentioned, the world was formed from something resembling the zero-point field, then clear dots and waves, and then dots that filled in and formed mass. Guided by the waves. There could have been—and probably was—a Big Bang occurrence, but that was not part of "The Knowledge"; however, "The Knowledge" supports that potential. All of this took place before the theory of the Big Bang could have been conceived. The mass that created the Big Bang formed from these simple beginnings, so the Big Bang was an effect—not a cause—of the universe's formation.

During the event on that November morning, I was provided "The Knowledge" of how dots and waves were attracted to each other and how they eventually filled the clear space with what, for lack of a better description, we label "energy" and "mass".

Here is where it gets complicated.

We do not scientifically, or in any other manner, understand the beginning of the universe as far as content and makeup. However, the message accompanying "The Knowledge" was that, for all intents and purposes, we stopped scientifically investigating the beginning of life with the splitting of the atom and the discovery of the deoxyribonucleic acid (DNA) double helix. At least I *thought* that science had given up until I was compelled to turn on the television to multiple affirmations of parts of the knowledge from documentaries, which prior to the arrival of the knowledge would have gone unnoticed by me. "Through the Worm Hole" narrated by Morgan Freeman for example; asking the pertinent questions but was falling short of the answers.

This next paragraph may be slightly confusing but later in the series of books it will make logical sense. I was conceived in 1952 the same year as an experiment was taking place to discover if a vacuum could produce substance and it was proven that it can. The "beginning of life" had seen a new "proven" potential. The universal knowledge base went to work creating a counter balance of knowledge in case this scientist did not appropriately convey the knowledge to the world; hang on, my apologies but it may have been the reason I was conceived. In addition, I was born healthy to an older mother (43) in the same month that scientist Watson and Crick proudly announced that the double helix mentioned above was "How Life Works". This simple wording set science on a research path that changed the path of discovery in a very detrimental way. Science was now focused on the cell to cure diseases and explain humanity rather than researching the space that surrounds the cell and contains our thought, feelings, beliefs and emotions for all of us. It is the communication vehicle for the cell. The missing piece of the puzzle is surrounding the cells and outside of the human body; not exclusively contained within the biological complexity. Water which is alive and has memory is the key component of the human body. Drink lots of water and read future books in this series for complex answers to the question of how life works.

The Bergabada Phenomenon

Bergabada Means "Nothing"

When I was a kid, I was walking with my two childhood friends, Danny and Bill, when one of us suddenly said, "Bergabada." We instantly understood that it meant "absolutely nothing." We started to use the word, knowing the rest of the school would think we had some secret code, and our school friends spent their time wondering how to crack it! We also added a finger snap, using both hands, which further confused the general population. It was a beautiful thing to watch, but you had to be there to understand the impact. Pretty much the same with understanding "The Knowledge" source.

It was all about nothing, and that is where the universe began: in a clear space with nothing in it. At least that is what one might think. The "Bergabada phenomenon" represents something that we have not yet labeled in human terms, mainly because we have not yet proven it scientifically; however, I stand firm in "The Knowledge" that it does exist. Please note the careful selection of the word "phenomenon" versus "theory."

This is not a theory. This is not Don's personal belief. This is knowledge direct from the source of all knowledge. Intended for all humanity. Period!

Note: The scientist just spit out his coffee and the skeptic went out to buy more printer ink:

"Hey, Tom. Did you read this? Some guy who grew up in farm country in western New York thinks he has "The Power of Knowing How Life Works"! Looks like our jobs as research scientists examining matter, atoms, and cells are obsolete!"

"He is probably another one of those religious-based theology majors. You can go back to reading your graphs and eating your donut, Bill!" I don't know Tom; this one sounds different than the rest!

Particle Energy Attraction

As I mentioned earlier, phenomena, which developed in the clear space, started attracting each other and forming solid matter (the fundamental base for the Law of Attraction), held in place by waves (the Bergabada phenomenon). The attraction of those two initial particles created how you live and work. You float through the universe on this wave, which is the carrier of the put-together particles. A particle soup of sorts, for lack of a better earthly word. The trillions of cells in your body independently and individually came from the same source. Filled with "water" to perpetuate their existence.

Billions of years later, because of the original shape of the phenomenon, the result was many big, solid balls floating around, all taking on different characteristics. This single interaction way back in the clear space formed the mass. The surrounding phenomenon (which, on earth, is referred to as "energy") controls each solid's existence.

Whatever word eventually names this interaction will describe the formation of the universe and the phenomenon that is still taking place, millions of light-years away, within and surrounding us all. Yes, the universe is expanding beyond known parameters.

As the solids were forming, the waves surrounding each solid continued to manage the solid through the growth process. The same phenomenon that surrounded each individual solid as it began its formation is the same phenomenon that exists around each object today—*including you.*

Humanity and every inch of space are part of the phenomenon. This explains how matter moves, how you function, and why we have natural disasters. It also explains physical relationships as well as relationships between businesses and customers, friends, sports teams and fans, police and criminals, people and professions, diseases and cures— everything related to everything! It explains why water is a massive part of earth.

I always smile when I hear an announcement that we have discovered a "new star" or an "unknown planet." *Of course, we have!* The phenomenon is constantly at work, creating new objects on a continuing basis. The phenomenon is always at work.

In this book, I refer to "positive" and "negative" energy; however, I am referring to the phenomenon. Since no one has yet discovered or scientifically proven the phenomenon, I am stuck with the traditional vocabulary. I must utilize overused terms of positive and negative energy, although that is not what the phenomenon is.

The Bergabada phenomenon is much more powerful than any known quantity labeled by humanity. Declaring that something has "energy" is a gross understatement of the phenomenon, which surrounds and sustains you. (I wish to clarify that although I use the word, "energy," in my writing, I use it frequently for lack of a better "earthly" word.) I have no other earthly word to use because the yet undiscovered phenomenon has not been named, and the makeup of what I refer to as energy has not yet been labeled.

In truth, the phenomenon that exists in the additional dimension that holds all thoughts, feelings, beliefs, emotions and knowledge cannot be measured as if it were "energy" as we currently know it. That's why it is yet undiscovered because we do not know how to measure it. At least now we know it exist, that is if I can get the right people to listen.

The Bergabada phenomenon is the beginning of your existence. If scientists try to measure the content of the phenomenon using traditional "energy" measurements they will not succeed. They must start to look at new ways of determining the actual makeup of the content contained within the phenomenon, and when they do, and people understand the makeup – which includes all thoughts, feelings, beliefs, emotions information and knowledge – then and only then, will we be able to visually see thoughts, feelings, knowledge and the beliefs that surround us all. I will repeat this until it is comfortable to all humanity.

I now know that, someday—once science has identified and discovered these items—humans will be able to see thoughts, feelings and beliefs before they enter the brain for processing. Vibrations (for lack of a better earthly word) transmit into your human processor (your brain); therefore, once you discover the items in a scientific environment and announce the existence of them, you create the potential to visually see them, much like electricity and telephone transmissions work but because they pass through a separate dimension we cannot see them as of yet, but we will because they already pass through the phenomenon. Imagine seeing a person's feeling or being able to see knowledge or information surrounding an individual! It's already there; we just have not yet confirmed it through scientific discovery and therefore we cannot see it.

At some point, we will be able to see the additional dimensions that hold the content because we will "believe" that they exist because science will have proven that they exist. No one would have imagined being able to call around the world until the telephone was exposed to the world and they believed it could work. Someday we will see those conversations or actually be able to telepathically communicate.

Additional Dimensions and Gravity

How the human body works is scientific fact; how the universe and humanity were created is religious theory; how science believes it started and how we function as humanity is theory as well. "The Knowledge" is now available to move forward.

The facts have actually arrived through this recent download of knowledge and at least one other time a couple of thousand years ago, but we misinterpreted the earlier knowledge through time and writings. I believe the facts have arrived many times in many forms, but we have chosen to discount the knowledge or totally ignore it.

The source for "The Knowledge" has always been the same: the universal knowledge base that resides in the fourth dimension where your thoughts, feelings, beliefs, emotions, knowledge, and information reside.

You cannot choose the source from which you will draw the knowledge. The source of "The Knowledge" is fixed, it is the universal consciousness that surrounds us, if you want to apply a superior being to your explanation of "The Knowledge" that is your prerogative. Note: You cannot say you want all of Einstein's knowledge because it has dispersed into the particle soup; what you attract is the focused result of what you intend to create utilizing a combination of data from the knowledge base.

If you believe that your knowledge, direction, inspiration, or ability to manifest comes from a certain source and it helps you feel good, then my rule of thumb is to *believe it*. You can hope that "The Knowledge" you receive comes from someone you respect or love, or one who has a particular talent, but in truth, the universe possesses *accumulated knowledge*. You process all particles, what you choose to keep is up to you.

"The Knowledge" surrounds you. It does not come from your gray matter. You are not preprogrammed to have knowledge. You manifest "The Knowledge" from the fourth dimension, which you cannot see because you do not believe that it exists, therefore, you cannot imagine what it looks like. Hence, you cannot visualize or conceptualize it.

The phenomenon that exists around you permeates the universe and acts as the storage device for unseen and unprocessed thoughts, feelings, beliefs, emotions, knowledge, and information. As I move through these real yet unseen "particles of thought" (for lack of a better earthly word), I now understand because of that life-changing November morning, I have actually received knowledge of the fourth dimension where thoughts, feelings, beliefs and emotions are stored before being processed.

The insights from that experience have guided me to understand that humanity has thus far misunderstood this entire process we call life. In truth, "The Knowledge" we seek, already exists from previous generations—both good and bad—and is available for you to manifest into your present life to create your personal reality.

Before "The Knowledge" arrived, I would have laughed at the notion of additional dimensions, but now, they are not only possible in theory, I can tell you that *they exist*. We live in one dimension of the universe, which contains multiple dimensions that may or may not function as we do. The clear space spawns a constant development of objects. Some exist in this dimension; some we cannot remotely relate to because they exist in other undiscovered dimensions. With the correct focus you can cross dimensions.

I do not want to get off in the weeds with sci-fi-like conversations about additional dimensions. When "The Knowledge" arrived, it carried the insight that everything is possible pertaining to the universe, based on the power of the phenomenon that we are discussing, but no specifics were provided on how to measure and quantify. These dimensions exist, but I did not recognize the specifics because the download was massive.

For simplicity's sake, let's use the word, "particles" to describe the knowledge pertaining to what happened to me while I was being provided information about the clear space. What arrived is that when the universe was formed, particles started attracting to other particles. As the attractions took place, objects were formed and processes were developed. The earth is an interesting result of the phenomenon because the core is hot, molten iron described by an earth term we call "gravity," surrounded by a hard surface on which we exist. Gravity is simply the phenomenon in its purest form, attracting us to the surface of the earth.

Various reactions developed—gasses and combinations of the particles—and created "life forms," as we have labeled them and the entire makeup of everything you see, feel, touch, and create. When water was created it carried the memory for life.

The reason we have not linked it together is that we have not yet defined the origin. Was it a gas or was it God? With this book, I am attempting to create the link but you would still have to accept the facts I am presenting as *your truth in order for this to make any useful sense.* If you do not, it is okay because the facts in this book will always remain *my truth.* Whether it be a gas or a God really does not matter for this discussion.

When we define the origin, we will better understand how everything fits together as one. However, we are "one" phenomenon and each day, when you walk around you are walking through the exact phenomenon as our origin. Your thoughts, makeup, and bodily movements are not movement at all in a traditional sense. In truth, you are suspended in the linked phenomenon in a defined dimension, which is yet undefined. That is why people have the power to manifest. We are the unknown phenomenon and the direct descendent from the phenomenon that developed at the beginning of the universe. What is next to you is identical to what you are; except you are visible.

The constant imbalance of the phenomenon explains the disruptions in our solar system, such as earthquakes, floods, tornados, and hurricanes—all natural disasters. Constant disruption of "vibrations" (for lack of a better earthly word) within the phenomenon causes these abnormalities to occur. As you move around in the phenomenon, changes in your thoughts and feelings disrupt the balance, like a pot of cold water boiling over when you add heat to it. Thoughts control the balance of life.

Universal Knowledge Base

The brain is a complex transceiver, transmitter, and transponder of components such as thoughts, feelings, beliefs, knowledge, and information. These components have accumulated over thousands of years from humanity coming and going. Acquired knowledge supplied by the cycle of life is contained in the phenomenon so that, over billions of years and with the deaths of billions of people over time, the phenomenon has acquired accrued knowledge. As we advance our thoughts we advance humanity. Technology has advanced because the universal consciousness has gotten smarter.

Accumulated knowledge from your physical time on earth and your accumulated positive and negative thoughts dissipate back into the universe—what I call the "universal knowledge base"—so future generations can draw from it. The fact that this knowledge base becomes smarter over time explains why technology moves at an ever-increasing pace. Think about the Morse code vs. today's email as a way to communicate.

When you accept The Power of Knowing How Life Works, you can easily tap into that knowledge (utilizing the Law of Attraction) and those thoughts and feelings from the universal database. This process fuels the Bergabada phenomenon.

The source—the universe—is simply a storage device or a hard drive, which allows you to retrieve information by utilizing your personal receiver and processor (the earthly word is your "brain"). So, your mind is merely a transceiver. It does not create thoughts, feelings and beliefs. It simply processes what we attract from the universal knowledge base, and then we take that end result and execute our lives with the knowledge that we have manifested. In other words, you can manifest the universal knowledge and build from it. We create our own reality!

If you understand the total process, it is easy to understand your dreams. Simply put, if you do not turn off your mind (the processor) at night, it just keeps working and processing extemporaneous information. That information has no particular focus, and therefore, causes people to be confused about their dreams. People try to analyze dreams as if they had a specific focus; they do not. Notice I used the word "specific". Most information that runs through the processor was attracted by you (manifested) so that it could be available to complete a focused thought at some time in your future. In a dream it was sent through the processor out of sequence without focus, and therefore, confuses the receiver. The information has meaning but because it is out of sequence you are incapable of understanding that meaning when you wake up.

Now here is the good news; all thoughts, knowledge, beliefs, feelings surround you and are part of the "particle soup" that makes us all up. So, if the content of the dream has significant meaning, you will reprocess the information through a "focused" thought and it will become "your" reality at some point. It will be however, in an unrecognizable form from the dream. It does still surround you, however.

I personally, very seldom dream. I go into a very deep REM sleep, shutting down the processor. I can do that for 10 minutes or 10 hours. However, when I lay quietly awake, my mind goes into rapid overdrive as I manifest knowledge routinely.

Another way to understand the idea of the mind operating like a processor is to look at children who are autistic. Kids with autism process information rapidly. Very seldom can they stop the processor or slow it down long enough to make sense of what they are processing, (much like your unexplained dreams). They experience a continuous flow of information from the universal data base through the processor.

More and more kids are being diagnosed with autism because of the increasing amount of knowledge available from the universal data base for them to process. If you have ever wondered about how an autistic person can be a savant or a musical prodigy, it is because they are able to focus on one point of interest while drawing powerful information through their processor; for example, an autistic pianist can gather up all of the knowledge, talent and understanding of past piano players and then become a superior player of that instrument. Make sense?

As for "The Knowledge", it is ever-present and always available to all of us. And when you pass on from your physical being, the manifested and accrued knowledge from your time on earth – such as from school, books, or seminars – recycles back into the universe. In this process, the universal database gets bigger and, yes, smarter!

This knowledge has circulated around objects for billions of years. Some of "The Knowledge" surrounds trees, plants, and animals—and, of course, humans—as well as other objects both visible and invisible, which emanated from the clear space. This includes, but is not limited to, solid objects such as mountains, rocks, tables, and chairs … *everything.*

When the car was invented, it began with an idea to eliminate horses from the transportation picture. "The Knowledge" was manifested from the universe on how to build the "horseless carriage." Hundreds of people deposited their knowledge into the universe, so the "collective accumulation" of knowledge was available to build the first car.

Think about all of the car advancements that have come along since then. People said that it would be nice to have a radio in the car or windshield wipers that hid themselves. Eventually, someone who had been looking for the answer manifested "The Knowledge" to build and advance the technology—in this case, probably a design engineer. They didn't intentionally manifest their answers; they didn't have to. They simply attracted the idea and then the universe helped them solve the problem, utilizing the consolidated knowledge particles it possesses.

That is how the Wright Brothers gathered enough information to fly. They saw a bird, which was part of the phenomenon and the universe, expanded their learning, and manifested knowledge from the universe. Before they knew it, they were airborne! Then, over the years, advancements and accumulated universal knowledge added to the original knowledge. Then, we had Boeing and Lockheed Martin!

Put it together: With advances in airplane design—from the Wright Brothers believing they could fly to Boeing employees building supersonic transports—the technology evolved because the available knowledge in the universe evolved. The reason the universe's knowledge evolved was because people died, dissipated into the universe, and the universe—for lack of a more sophisticated explanation—became smarter over time, caused by the deposit of accumulated collective knowledge into the phenomenon that created the universe. I know those that feel that books provided the knowledge I will not argue, books are simply an advanced rapid way for people to gain knowledge.

By refueling the universe with knowledge from those who have died, we become smarter and smarter. "The Knowledge" is available for all people to manifest. Today, technology seems to be moving at an unbelievable pace and, by now, you should be able to understand why. Thousands of people die, along with the thoughts and knowledge that advance humanity. Then, an individual or group manifests "The Knowledge" and creates new and advanced technology, each time more sophisticated.

The key component is that the requester knows they can—and believe they *will*—find the answers. I personally never wanted to invent a radio or hide windshield wipers, but someone did. They must have *because it was done.*

We are all linked—as living, breathing, physical beings, and as solids, liquids, and gases in the dimension we call "earth"—through the phenomenon fueled by water. Through that link, we have multiplied our existence and cultivated what we now know as "humanity." Don't underestimate this, it is powerful stuff!

We have defined the confines within which we exist as the "universe," so every "thing" within those confines is linked. Even though you cannot see or touch your thoughts or knowledge (yet), they obviously exist and are linked to your beginning and continued existence; therefore, you have the capability to utilize thoughts, feelings, beliefs and knowledge that exist in the universe in ways that you have never conceived.

The universe cannot determine right from wrong or good from evil. It cannot make decisions for you. It can only supply you with solutions from its accumulated knowledge; however, you and only you can determine what to ask for.

"Okay, Don. I want to be smart, so why didn't I get 1500 on my SATs?"

The real answer is that the person asking this question, from a very early age, manifested other avenues for their life, while the person whom we call a "genius" focused on knowledge manifestation.

When you embrace "The Power of Knowing How Life Works", it will change your life. After that November morning, I no longer believe that we have a preset destiny. I know now that only I can determine my future by setting goals and accepting into my life the type of thought particles (energy) that will support my life in a positive way.

You manifest everything in your life, including "The Knowledge", which is available from the universal consciousness. Until that event, I didn't understand. When the clock hit 6:24 a.m., everything started falling into place. My lifelong unanswered questions started to become perfectly clear. I understood the "whys" of many of what I had previously thought to be the coincidences and incidences in my life, and gained a sense of tranquil peace. If you walk around in neutral; wake up, there is a whole new life ahead of you regardless of your age or environment in which you live.

I attracted my wife into my life to be with me for what has become 40 years of my 59-year journey, which eventually led me here, right now, and allowed me to place this book in your hands. My wife is supportive, but there is something more powerful working. I realize now that I had utilized "The Power of Knowing How Life Works" my entire life without even knowing it. From age 10 I have been in training to receive it.

My wife often asks me what role she will play in the future distribution of "The Knowledge". My answer is simple: the same role you played in getting me to this point after the universe assigned us to spend our lives together, so you could keep me on track to train and prepare for the distribution of "The Knowledge". I call it a "vision," but our marriage was a mandate from the universe. Fortunately, we were matched pretty well!

Although I did not understand my life as it unfolded; my training was right on target. I made choices, but I had help. By visualizing, I had manifested the universe to open the doors along the way to get me where I wanted to go. All this started when I was a 10-year-old child, or possibly even younger. Keep in mind that I couldn't even spell the word "manifesting" at age 10, let alone know what it meant. However, I now know that it was *exactly* what I was doing. The traditional thinkers may refer to it as praying.

On reflection, having stood on that Arizona golf tee at age 20, I realize that I attracted *all* of it into my life: the job, the experiences, and the plan. Then, after the plan wasn't working anymore, I sat in the storage shed with a gun to my temple, trying to decide if my life was worth living. I manifested the bad from the same source.

I know, without qualification or hesitation, that when I stopped calling upon the energy for visualization and attraction, my ability to positively move forward went dormant. For the first time in my life, I was in neutral mode. When negative events started to happen, I went the wrong way. I attracted more negative in my life, and it continued until I ended up in the shed. I had to experience that in order to understand.

Even though my emotional state was a mess, I had no real intention of following through or I would have completed the task. The universe wanted me to get to that state of collapse so I could help people who have reached total despair in their lives. Without the experience of sitting in that shed, under those real-life circumstances, I would never have been able to understand the complete picture. It was part of the training.

The insights that arrived that morning following the knowledge download made purpose of the arrival of "The Knowledge," crystal clear. I received the answer I had been asking the universe my whole life. "The Knowledge" provided me with *The Power of Knowing How Life Works.*

Four Important Points worth repeating:

1. The Bergabada phenomenon is the same phenomenon that was present at the beginning of the universe. It was nothing and turned into particle soup.

2. The Bergabada phenomenon is where your thoughts, feelings, beliefs, knowledge, and information are stored. The brain is merely a processor; it does not generate these things. You can manifest them, acknowledge them, and then accept them as you wish. The most powerful focus should be on belief; make sure it is positive.

3. You have access to ALL of the knowledge of the universe on a 24/7 basis. Every snippet of data, and every thought, feeling, or idea that has ever been expressed, plus more, is always available to you. YOU and only YOU control the outcome of your thoughts as you convert them into your reality.

4. "The Knowledge" is located in the fourth dimension of the universe. In your three-dimensional world, it may be hard to understand that something you

cannot see, residing within and surrounding you, is the key component to your existence.

The God Particle

After working on this book and pondering the insights for well over a year, and reviewing my overwhelming experience, I had this crazy yet powerful impulse on Mar. 6, 2011, to go home in the middle of the afternoon to write more. It was not normal for me to go home at that time, and with that sense of urgency, but the feelings were overwhelming.

"What's wrong?" my wife called out as I almost ran out of our retail store.

I could not explain. It is simply a powerful feeling that I have had before.

I got home, fully intending to write, but was instead compelled to turn on the television. Right there, in front of me, right at that moment, was another affirmation. The History International channel was airing the *New Big Bang* feature program. I had no idea what it was going to be about, but I have learned to accept these interruptions in my schedule as continued training. These types of instances are routine in my life.

It talked about a large group of scientists—from Europe and all over the world—who were working on an underground project called LHC—CERN (Large Hadron Collider, built by the European Organization for Nuclear Research), encompassing 12 countries in cooperation with each other and working on particle accelerator collider physics. It was another affirmation that "The Knowledge" was pure. I had never heard of this work before, had just been pondering my writing about the clear space, and then along came the affirmation. Could particles penetrate mass? Yes, neutrinos can do that.

On the program, they mentioned the "God particle" the absolute beginning of it all—the particle they know exists but have not yet found. (Keep looking, guys ... it's there!) When I heard this, I smiled, because I knew they understood at least some of my journey, and someday I hope to meet these scientists. I am not smart enough to have even remotely come up with this stuff myself. They are trying to create the circumstances of the Big Bang; they must look at conditions before the Big Bang.

As I mentioned earlier, the phenomenon started from a clear space—literally from nothing. If it started from nothing, then wouldn't some source *have* to be responsible for the very first fractional ounce of the beginning? Scientists will have to determine the makeup of the first chemical activity (or whatever it was). God will be the answer to that question for many, but my insights tell me that we should keep looking.

Some "clear" and transparent phenomenon—possibly a clear, odorless gas—started the chain reaction, which took billions of years to become visible. It is entirely possible that it resides in another dimension. Science is on the right path with examination of zero-point fields and the LHC particle accelerator, but the discovery by Watson and Crick of the double helix in 1953, and its association with DNA, tossed science off track. Particles smaller than atoms, unseen before are the answers to look for.

Watson, Crick, and Me

James D. Watson and Francis Crick—two British scientists, of whom I had never heard—announced that they had discovered the double helix of DNA and proclaimed it the foundation to how life works in 1953 the same month and year that I was born.

Why was I compelled to look this up in the first place? What does it have to do with me? I had absolutely no connection or interest in any of this before my November 2009 experience. What does it have to do with this story? Maybe nothing … maybe *everything*. Maybe I was conceived to protect against a misinterpretation over time.

The universe provides me with the clarity to the insights with real-life answers, as I need them. Prior to the arrival of "The Knowledge", I could not even spell "quantum physics." The only reason I passed chemistry and biology in school was the fact that they needed me on the football team. (Okay, I passed on my own merits, but just barely.)

Since my experience, people have sent me small excerpts from books or participated in conversations with me confirming what a particular insight was intended to mean, just so I could figure out how to explain it to you. People come into my life from all angles, including, but not limited to, just walking in my door at our retail establishments. They often drop off an article or a book relating to a previous conversation that we may have had or to look at me and walk away shaking their head.

It gets spooky at times but I look at each person as additional knowledge and smile.

My wife is still amazed at how I continually get into off-the-wall conversations with perfect strangers. To me, the conversations make perfect sense. The universe sends these people to affirm my direction. I knew nothing about zero-point fields or of Watson and Crick until two unrelated friends of mine provided books for me to read.

"Here, Don. For some reason, we are supposed to deliver these to you."

I usually do not have to read much of a book to find the paragraph or two that jumps out at me and affirms a particular insight that I might be working on that day.

The "Wow" Factor: What Science Missed

I am clear that an unknown, undiscovered phenomenon exists throughout the universe. "The Knowledge" contains insights that will act as the catalyst for scientists to shift their thinking and allow for the discovery of this phenomenon.

Traditional, earthly words such as "energy," "vibrations," and "particles" are used to describe our existing knowledge as to how life works. These words do not apply to the Bergabada phenomenon. These earthly words have kept scientists from discovering the phenomenon. The reason is when they are trying to measure energy they are missing "it".

The phenomenon that I describe is the same process that created the universe billions of years ago. It exists within, between, and surrounding every mass in the universe, including all of humanity. I repeat this over and over as it is the key to life.

Universal laws, such as the Law of Attraction, and your daily thoughts and actions are contained within this powerful phenomenon. Every aspect of mass on earth relates directly back to the beginning of the universe and the phenomenon that surrounds us. When we discover, label, and identify the phenomenon, we will solve every issue in the world and every disease that exists. "The Knowledge" was delivered will we listen?

This is not science fiction. This is a true understanding at a fundamental level that provides "The Power of Knowing How Life Works".

How Can Science Benefit from "The Knowledge"?

The purpose of "The Knowledge" as delivered to me is to encourage scientists to keep looking for the answer to what comprises the phenomenon. The answer is clearly in the universe for scientists to attract. Quite honestly, the makeup of the phenomenon is not that important as long as we know how it works and, more importantly, that it exists.

Water is a key component. I do not proclaim to be a scientist. I cannot argue with any expert who will question my basic approach to how it works. I am merely stating the insights of "The Knowledge" that arrived that incredible morning.

When a physical being is formed, the surrounding phenomenon has given that person the ability to attract particles from the universe as well as be influenced by their immediate environment, which is what makes each of you different. You are comprised of particle soup, but the influences that surround your life pull create different solutions.

DNA identified me at birth as an individual. When the sperm met the egg and conception took place, my DNA formed. The sperm and the egg are comprised of cells, which carried with them my stamp of identity and helped the union take place. The surrounding phenomenon fueled the learning and growth processes aided by water.

The reason you are different is that, when the sperm and the egg meet, right at that precise moment in time, more particles (the phenomenon) surrounds and joins them. The roadmap—

DNA—gives you individuality; the particles (phenomenon), which surrounds the area, immediately begins to form your personality as your reality is created.

As you grow in the womb, your personality, your size, and even your demeanor start to develop based on the particles surrounding you from the very beginning. Whatever your biological parents attracted during your conception is available to you; however, you can start attracting your own phenomenon loaded with knowledge as needed. You are not doomed to failure because of your environment or history. You may, however, be doomed if you cannot adjust your future vision into a positive outcome.

Throughout your entire physical existence, the particles that surrounds you is the reality that you are attracting into your life and that forms your future—that's why your DNA is unique—but your personalities can be different or similar. For example, twins think alike because they were conceived in the same environment at the same time.

A Simple Reminder

The discovery of the double helix of DNA was in 1953—the year I was born—and the significance to my birth is interesting. If you want to take this to the next level, I will be happy to discuss the potential that the universe created me so I could one day help people get back on track after the discovery of the double helix.

How, you ask?

The universe has provided me with a simple reminder to scientists all over the world to keep looking for the makeup of the phenomenon that surrounds us, and for people all over the world to start manifesting a better life for themselves and everyone else. Driven by the fact that we are all linked together through the phenomenon.

If you manifest your own good life, and everyone else in the world manifests a good life, then you are inadvertently manifesting a better life for everyone. You cannot manifest for others; however, you can influence others' lives with your own manifestations if they are stronger. Thoughts play a major role in the survival of humanity

There are thousands of examples where one party is in neutral mode and the other party dominates the result with a stronger thought (manifestation) process. For example, if a criminal or an abuser inflicts their will on unsuspecting others who have no focus on their own protection, the perpetrator wins. If parents have not taught their children to think for themselves, and the parents always wanted their child to go to a particular school, the child is in neutral mode and the parents' manifestations (wishes) take priority over the outcome. Same with political and religious leaders, they dominate you serve.

The answer is simple: Implementable solutions to a good life are possible if you understand "how life works". The phenomenon is universal and the same for everyone and everything on the planet. Secret societies have used this knowledge for years.

"If it is that simple," you may ask, "why hasn't everyone implemented it? Why don't we know how it works already?" People that know control the world, get it?

I can hear the lady in Michigan scream, "We *do* know how it works. It works because God set the plan." Our lives are driven by destiny....they are not!

I respect that viewpoint. It is the reason I asked you to store and preserve your traditional thoughts in the box in the beginning of the book. I know those thoughts are precious to millions of you. How is it working so far? If it is all good; then great!

I am simply sharing "The Knowledge", which will vary in a big way from traditional thoughts. That is the purpose of the book and the reason I received "The Knowledge". Not everyone wants to believe that the solution is so simple; those who understand it have kept it a secret for hundreds of years so that you serve them.

So why did it take 56 years (the elapsed time between 1953 when Watson and Crick discovered the double helix associated with DNA and the first writing of this book)? It has to do with our perceived "time" here on earth. Fifty-six years is the blink of an eye in universal time. You would not have believed anything else at an earlier delivery point because the double helix explained so many things.

Now, you are ready to rethink the beginning of your existence.

Time and Future Predictions

There is no "time" element. Time is man-made, so traditional time references mean nothing to the universal big picture. There is no universal time; dates, hours, clocks, or calendars. These measurements exist only in man's eyes; we created them as data points. When the universe was created the beginning of the knowledge base began and grew as things lived and died. We are fortunate because the universe created water, a place for knowledge to accumulate and in turn there is a synergy among us. The universe had no set pattern; it just created a way for us to communicate and linked us together.

Nostradamus (1503–1566), the French apothecary and reputed seer, made predictions of events taking place before they happened. In a certain dimension, he saw up to the year 3037, but the timeframe from which he looked was so fast in universal time that it was a flash to him. His life time compared to the age of the universe was a flash.

Nostradamus was able to see events, but they had no name because humanity had not yet named them. He received a download from the universe and, like me, wrote what he remembered in that scene, but the universe is not divided into time. He divided his thoughts into packets of 10 quatrains, or stanzas, which he called a "century," and then over an earthly timeframe as they seemingly occurred in history we have applied what he saw to instances that happened in those timeframes. In this framework, his visions looked like he was predicting the future. When in reality he was seeing ahead in time instantaneously into the dimension we refer to as the future. His processor just ran faster than ours and he caught up with himself within his own life time frame.

Earth Time vs. Universal Time

As I mentioned earlier, the two occurrences of my paralysis were 30 years apart. In "universal time," 30 earth years compared to billions of universal years is a snap of your fingers. This thought process also applies to why it took 47 years to get an answer to a very focused question. I actually received my answer instantaneously after asking.

When people say, "Time is passing fast," they have no idea how close they are to the reality of the universe. When I say that my experience locked me into 6:24 for a very long time, that process was necessary in order to supply billions of years of universal history within that one minute of earthly time. Keeping in mind that there is no universal time our lives go by in a flash of universal experience.

Between 6:00 and 6:23 a.m. that morning, I experienced the exchange of my existing traditional knowledge and accumulated learning dispersed back into the universe, which prepared me for the new download of knowledge. In simplistic terms, "Out with the old and in with the new!" the clearing of the hard drive in today's terms.

Earth time is man-made—a measurement of "nothing" in relation to the universe. Universal experiences are measured in light-years, which are also man-created measurements. None of it means anything in relation to the phenomenon that surrounds you and provides the power that drives your life and existence.

Just a few decades ago, the life expectancy was 15 to 30 years because that is what people believed. It rose to 40, then 50, and now we assume 75 to 85 years for an average life span because we expect to live that long. If everyone believed and focused on living to 150, we probably could do it! The answers on how to do it will arrive when the focus becomes powerful enough. The issue then becomes this; no one before us put those thoughts into the Universe for us to manifest so how do we do it? We build a new reality from the existing thoughts, just like we advance technology through particle collaboration. OK, that will be in about book #7 to much for the scope of this book.

During that life-changing minute, I had no idea why 6:24 was significant. I now know that it coincided with the moment I emptied stress, traditional beliefs, and excess baggage from around me and cleared the memory of non-essential data points. It was scary but, at the same time, very calming. I was ready to receive the download which would contain "The Power of

Knowing How Life Works". What was to follow the first 23 minutes was one earthly minute of overwhelming and powerful transition of knowledge.

Let me take a moment to discuss universal consciousness because it is so critically important to our ability to manifest a powerful life. All of the earthly words that we have composed to guide our lives such as destiny, fate, luck and "it was meant to be" will be disregarded over time as we begin to believe and conceive the knowledge from the universal data base. Small yet to be discovered particles make up the universal consciousness that surrounds us. These particles contain your thoughts, feelings, beliefs and emotions. Why do I repeatedly stress these points throughout this book, because you process knowledge over and over again until you resonate with its importance and this is critically important for everyone to grab onto. These undiscovered particles make up everything including water. Structured water is the backbone of our beginning as a human form. If you are of the mind that GOD created water I will not dispute that; it is just not part of this important discussion.

Birth and Death

It Is All Around You

In my early years, during those warm summer nights under the stars, I asked the question, "How does this all work?" Then, throughout my adult life, I asked the same questions at different locations across the United States. Because of the six company moves that I had manifested, I was able to approach the universe with my questions from all corners of the country. I was in training to learn about diversity, culture and life as we know it.

I used to ask my childhood friends, who had died at early ages, as well as my parents, who had passed on, for guidance. I was simply looking for answers and they were a logical source (at least I *thought* they were).

Now I know that the particles (for lack of a better earthly word) of those who previously walked the earth surround us: prophets, poets, inspirational leaders, and all the people from your past. Their collective knowledge and particles are dispersed in the universe and available at any time. You just cannot be sure whose knowledge you obtain.

As new knowledge pours back into the universe through the death of generations, the universe gets smarter as the cycle of life advances "The Knowledge". When you die, the physical form dissipates into the universe and back into the phenomenon we mistakenly refer to as "energy." All of the good, positive energy with which you lived, any bad negative energy which you carried to death, and the thoughts, feelings and beliefs, plus "The Knowledge" (particles) which you learned during your comparatively short time on earth are included in that transition. Yes, you will return as particles.

When all of that knowledge (particles) dissipates back to the universe, it is available for the next generation to attract or use to refuel the sun and stars; fill voids in the energy balance; or be attracted by plants, animals, or fish to continue the cycle. Along with the positive and negative energy, the energy we call "knowledge," "memory," and "logic" goes back into the universe and is available for someone or some process to reuse. If you are an old sole you have manifested knowledge from many years ago.

Utilizing the Law of Attraction; "The Knowledge", thoughts, feelings, beliefs and emotions surround you throughout your life, so the surrounding knowledge is also released at death. Now that you are thinking out of the box, you can think completely through the process. As you get smarter, the universe gets smarter, and people can draw from each other both during and after your physical existence because it is all the same phenomenon. Many people know that the Law of Attraction works, few can explain how. The beginning of the universe is when the Law of Attraction went to work.

For example, if someone needs help, and has someone to help them, it is possible for the person in "need" to attract the particles that surround the person helping. That explains why teachers are so tired at the end of a school day or therapists are drained at the end of a session. The phenomenon surrounds you, and your connection with others determines who ends up with the energy particles based on need and focus.

Maybe I knew none of the people who supplied "The Knowledge" from which I draw; however, in reality, as you seek answers in your daily life, you should not be concerned with whomever or whatever powerful source is supplying them. If I need a realignment of my direction, or a boost of positive energy to keep my life on track, I now know where to get it. I simply walk through happy people or manifest good feelings.

A New Being

When theorists say, "We are all one," they actually offer a true statement. When all of your "essence" blends or dissipates back into the universe, only to regroup again and again in a different formation as a new "body," then that body will contain parts of everyone else's soul (for lack of a better earthly word) as well as yours, which, of course, is made up of the mix. According to the Law of Attraction, you will naturally attract the positive or negative vibration based on where your predecessors left off in their previous life. However, make no mistake YOU and only YOU are in control of how you turn out.

Every individual is a new being at the time of conception. Available to that new being is the phenomenon that surrounds them and every aspect and body part. Through the Law of Attraction, the newly conceived life form has the ability to attract "their" make-up from the universal knowledge base, which comprises thoughts, feelings, beliefs, emotions and knowledge from the dissipated previous owners and which is stored in the phenomenon that surrounds them. Water has memory which means you have memory.

With the population "expanding" as it is, the likelihood of the dissipation ending up supplying humanity is great (that is, more people are being born than dying), but the imbalance in the phenomenon because of this occurrence and our imbalance of thoughts is the cause of the natural disasters being created. Natural disasters are simply the adjustment of the phenomenon as shifts and imbalances occur in the universe (more specifically, in the dimension in which we live in the universe). More in future books!

Is it time for a glass of wine? At least go get my favorite beverage…..WATER!

What Happens When You Die?

If I were on the radio right now, the phones would light up and the station manager would knock on the locked door, demanding silence! I am reminded of Robin Williams in *Good Morning, Vietnam* when, as a radio DJ, he was broadcasting against policy. (In this case, my words are against traditional values.) Or are they, they may align perfectly if you are open to possibilities and apply "The Knowledge" without prejudice or judgment.

Maybe I should have branded the book, *The Power of Knowing How Life and Death Works*; however, when you know how life works, you can then understand the total cycle of life *and* death.

This is *my story.* I will share it, but you do not have to accept it in any way.

Still with me? Let's continue!

Death is a continuation of life in a different dimension. The cycle of the universe, which of course includes death, continues. I was provided "The Knowledge" of what happens when we die. It is not opinion or theory. The universe allowed me to manifest these facts for you. If you are looking for affirmations of Heaven and Hell you will need to utilize another source. My only responsibility is to share what was delivered.

When you die, particles are released in either a unified or a dispersed form. If the mental state of the individual is positive, and the circumstances surrounding the end of the physical form were positive (in lay terms, it was "time" to die and the natural life cycle was complete), the particle energy is released and dispersed as positive energy.

The converse is also true. If a person dies with negative energy, they may not die in peace and may linger in a less dispersed form until they can rest in peace. This insight was very clear and will account for people experiencing the presence of ghosts or aberrations, or explain people's ability to recall the energy from a person who has passed. This I assume, has always been the claim of misunderstood mediums and channels.

Often, people left behind after someone dies have powerful thoughts, which they do not let go of until they achieve resolution or come to terms with the death. They actually *keep alive* for a short time the energy of their loved ones who have passed. The powerful need of those left behind to grieve for the loss of their loved ones does not let the particles dissipate into the universe because the Law of Attraction is confused. Their powerful grief feelings disrupt the entire process at least for a short time.

During your existence in the physical form, it is up to you to control how you will spend eternity. This point is critical in understanding "The Power of Knowing How Life Works". When you leave your earthly being, make no mistake: You will be back but not in the same particle energy form. However, the energy with which you leave is the same "type" of energy that you disperse into the universe for someone else to attract.

You return as thoughts, feelings, beliefs and emotions to assist the next generation with their existence. That is why I mentioned above that if someone feels like an "old soul," for example, he or she very well may have attracted a larger percentage of available particles from many years ago. However, not everyone will feel like an old soul; they have simply attracted particles from a more modern source. Criminals attract hate, humanitarians attract compassion and so it continues.

When you die and then you are attracted by a living entity, you will be part of that physical form but mixed with all the particle soup attracted by that person at that time. There is no free ride, if you live your life with hate and die you do spend eternity as you left. There is no hell but you will leave as you believe and return in the particle form you create while living. That is the reason to live a good life, filled with love and compassion.

I understand that many traditionalists are simply going to refuse to think out of the box. It is okay; however, they will not possess "The Power of Knowing How Life Works." Our lives are powerful masses of particles chose and process them wisely.

Energy is Pure

When you die, energy is released in a pure state. When it comes back into use by the universe, it comes back as particles that you attract. It is not black, white, or brown; not a Democrat or Republican; not a Catholic, Jew, or Muslim. They are simply particles without prejudice— they are however, positive or negative—*period! Your thoughts are what determine your reality. You and only You chose what to store.*

When I use the term "when you die," I am talking about every aspect of the phenomenon, such as trees and mountains, plants and animals, liquid, gas, solids and physical beings. For example, you know that a tree is alive because it takes water and carbon dioxide to live and gives off oxygen for you to live. If you cut down the living tree, it no longer produces oxygen or uses your water supply. You chop it down, make lumber, and build a building. The building burns to ashes, and the carbon dioxide from the fire goes to the universe. The particles may be attracted by the remaining trees to continue living and, in turn, produce oxygen for you to breathe. Or you could take on the particles in some form as well. The particle soup is amazing stuff.

We are linked because the phenomenon surrounds everything. The particles, which is available for you to attract, is from everyone on the planet and everything in the universe—whether you are living or dead—regardless of political, economic, racial, or religious beliefs. You have the ability to attract the answers, which are cumulatively available, and make the choices that will give you the life you desire.

Death and Attraction

When you die you join the particles deposited from the past life of everything, which has dissipated and dispersed throughout the universe and you become part of the soup. That explains why cumulative knowledge from everyone is constantly filling the universe.

Scientists will want to use the word "energy," but the separation between the concepts of energy and the phenomenon must remain in order to continue to look for the source. Based on your traditional beliefs, you can only imagine the forms or substances in earthly terms such as "particles" and "energy"; however, it is much greater than what earthly terms can describe. Scientist knows that there is something they cannot find; they are looking and soon will identify and quantify the missing piece of the puzzle. Then we will believe and conceive "The Knowledge".

Your thoughts, feelings, beliefs and emotions become part of the phenomenon and are available for "something" in the universe to utilize as needed. You may be attracted by the sun in order to refuel its brilliance. You may become a source of energy for a star. You may be attracted by some form of humanity to supply knowledge, power, or thought. You may be attracted by a plant or animal but you will be back. The fun part is you will disperse into many different venues and be part of many lives.

The universal Law of Attraction has its roots in the phenomenon, which created the universe, so the ability for all things to attract is fundamental and the source for what they attract is available from the phenomenon. When you die, you become part of that phenomenon, and so it continues. Forgive my redundancy of words, it is intentional.

Billions of Bodies

As contradictory as it sounds, my download of knowledge clearly defined an "unknown phenomena." Humanity describes it as "energy." Millions, even billions, of people have died around the world over the span of time that our world has been in existence. Those people, for thousands of years, have expelled their energy back into the universe. More accurately, the phenomenon, which created them, returns to its original form. All energy released into the universe, from humanity and for billions of years, is available to you.

Where do you think these billions of physical bodies ended up? They are not floating around the universe in a visible form, such as the myth of floating ghosts, which we have created in an image that looks like humanity. No such visuals or dimensions exist. If you have seen a ghost, you *wanted* to see it, but it has long since dispersed into the universe. I keep open the possibility that we may have aberrations in the dissipation process that would leave a person's energy together forever but none of my knowledge confirmed that potential. I will not dispute Angels or Ghost or white lights or tunnels.

Those who have had near-death experiences did not die; if they had, their thoughts, feelings, beliefs, emotions and knowledge would have dissipated into the universe. An organ may have stopped working for a short time, or they may have had an interruption of consciousness, but they didn't die. They merely had temporary interruptions in the processing that takes place in the brain. I am not saying they did not have the experience, my knowledge simply explains they did not die.

Although my experience was extremely unusual, nothing resembled the miraculous lights or euphoric visions always described with typical near-death or returning-from-death experiences. Because I now know how it works, however, I am confident that these other types of events are very real experiences and should not be discounted until proven otherwise. Please no emails concerning near death experiences.

Think of it this way: Energy particles make up all living things. (The scientific terms are "cells," "atoms," and "molecules.") Imagine that billions of people release energy as they die and dissipate that energy back into the universe to keep humanity going. This is not a divine providence or destiny; it just happens to be that way.

When something living dies, or is killed or harvested, such as a plant or a tree, the energy is again transferred as needed into the universe or, in some cases, if attracted by a living being, it may even be transferred directly into the "consumer" of that particular plant or tree. Maybe that dissipated energy was used to create a flower, an insect, a fish, or a bird, or to replenish the sun, the stars, moons, planets, and ... yes ... *even you!*

If you want an example of the recycling of things other than humans, remember our example earlier of old housing. When a house burns, where do you think the lumber from the living tree, which built the house, goes? It's the same for the erosion of mountains or lava. As rock burns, water evaporates and goes back into the phenomenon that created it. Sometimes it takes years but, in universal time, it takes only minutes.

Early Native American culture believed this in the way they lived. Someone gave them "The Knowledge" and it got lost in the shuffle of life, or in the language translation, but the elders know what I am describing. Secret societies have kept control through the use of "The Knowledge" and quite honestly have kept you enslaved in your lives.

Death and Choice

If you would accept how life and death worked, if you believed that you could make your own decisions on how to live your life and if you knew that the decisions you made affected the results in your life, you would have implemented a master plan and been happy with your life as it is—not just in general, but in all aspects. The choices you make in your life determine how you end up just before you die. We never know exactly when we are going to die so living a good positive life is really the only assurance that you will leave this life and join eternity and the particle soup as a positive contribution.

This is a fun time to ask you a question that by now you should be able to answer. Is life composed of fate or free will? Thoughts are powerful and you and only you choose your reality.

The reality is that we will all die someday, "The Knowledge" provides many interesting aspects as to the process of death. "The Knowledge" leaves open the possibility that humanity has a choice as to when we die. The power of belief is an overwhelmingly powerful tool in the process. If you spend your life looking at a calendar assuming that you are a certain age and that because of that calendar you start to count how many years have seemingly flown by and how many on some contrived average calculation that we have left you start to build your reality around that earthly time frame. "The Knowledge" has explained that there is no time in the universe and therefore it is our belief that our life expectancy is pre-determined by thoughts as opposed to any real biological depletion. We simply tell our cells we are getting old and the calendar confirms it and we believe it and then it becomes our reality. It will be fun to work on shifting our thoughts on age.

Negative Environmental Influences

Crimes and Retribution

I recently paused in front of the television to watch a segment about my local county jail. Two hundred new arrivals went through their doors in an average evening. *Wow!* Two hundred people felt compelled to be destructive to themselves or to others in one county in one evening. Now that you are familiar with how it works, figure out the influence that the jail environment will have on their behavior and thoughts. They are surrounded by what?

The actions inside this facility were baffling. It was a chilling example of humanity versus humanity in an attempt to gain superiority—the true definition of war—only this was in my own backyard. Unfortunately, we have learned to accept this behavior as the norm. When we put criminals with criminals we create criminals.

As I mentioned before, those left behind after someone dies often have powerful thoughts that do not let go until they achieve resolution or come to terms with the death. They actually *keep the energy alive* with their thoughts, which are powerful enough, for example, to exact retribution on a perpetrator. The thought of retribution solves crimes.

Let me explain. A perpetrator goes into neutral mode (unless, of course, they are a serial perpetrator) and becomes complacent at some point after a crime thinking that they have gotten away with the crime, while the grieving family or determined police officer stays focused. When this happens, the universe gives the knowledge to "the focused," and that is how we solve crimes. The one who wants to solve the crime has "stronger" focus or will power than the one who committed the crime. That is why, on cold cases, you often find retired detectives working on the same case for 30 years; eventually, they solve it, or at least see justice of some kind on the perpetrator as the perpetrator slips into neutral mode and gets focused on something other than not getting caught.

For those committing crimes, you can laugh this off, but rest assured—or, better yet, *rest uneasy*—that, when the citizens of the world truly understand "The Power of Knowing How Life Works," they will track you down and lock you in prison for your crimes. Even if they don't catch you, but someone wants justice, he or she will manifest it because the crime will weigh heavily on your mind and you will self-inflict punishment. If not, your own self-destruction will be your demise because you will focus on your crime and worry about being caught, in other words you will feel guilty, which will assist those who are looking for you. It is also possible that someone will want you to be caught and will catch you. You cannot escape you will either wear yourself out or self-implode.

When we teach law enforcement officers how to focus on cases, the world will change rapidly as it relates to crime. The combination of the perpetrator feeling guilty and the law enforcement community wanting to catch them will utilize the Law of Attraction and they will be caught. It works. Read the newspapers: Bad guys eventually go to prison. There was a female detective in Arizona who stayed focused on a serial killer for many years. She solved the crimes using the principles contained in "The Power of Knowing How Life Works." She did not know she was utilizing the process; she just did it and eventually the perpetrator was killed.

There is no heaven or hell; however, there is much more detail concerning the eternal continuation of your existence. People who commit heinous crimes against society and catastrophic harm against others, without changing the way they think and live before they die, will spend eternity as negative energy.

It is about positive or negative energy—not heaven or hell. I know the traditional thought is that a murderer or rapist would go to hell. The authors of that "big book" got it almost right, but the labels are wrong.

Review: If the energy surrounding the physical form is negative (such as in the case of a tragic or a sudden, unexpected death), then the energy stays united and is in the universe for an extended period of time until resolution is somehow completed and the energy breaks up and disperses. Eventually, however, the energy—positive and negative—created when someone dies is dispersed, and the cycle of life is completed as the physical form transforms into eternal energy.

If hate consumes you and you want to inflict pain, you probably will. It works both ways. Hopefully, if you are in a negative mode, someone will stop you by manifesting the law-abiding side of the equation more strongly than you will manifest your hate and crime thoughts. That is why some criminals are caught on the scene and others get away. If a law enforcement team wants to catch the bad guys, and the bad guys are careless or have remorse for what they have done, then the police are going to win every time.

If you have committed a crime and think you have gotten away with it, think again. Be prepared to spend eternity as negative energy and, when you finally understand how this all works, know you have dispersed negative energy back in the universe for someone in the future to attract.

That "someone" may be your own child or sibling.

Thoughts about the Death Penalty

If someone murders another human being and many witnesses saw it, I used to believe in the "eye for an eye" theory of the death penalty:

"Hang 'em on the spot!" (Hey, I was a country boy.)

However, now that I have been provided "The Power of Knowing How Life Works" I have reevaluated my position and thought. If a person kills another in hate and anger, they possess negative energy. It surrounds them and is the core of their makeup. Knowing that energy goes back into the universe, and then we kill a person who possesses negative energy—in this case, a killer—we are releasing negative energy into the universe.

Now, make no mistake where I am going with this. I do feel strongly that we should lock up murderers and throw away the key— but along the way we should *try* to turn them around to think positively; otherwise, we are just releasing negative energy into the universe for someone else to attract. It really is that simple.

I am not suggesting that we rehabilitate killers and release them back into society. If they committed an unspeakable act of violence, they indeed need to pay for it with hard labor.

Instead, I am proposing the rehabilitation of a killer for the sake of future humanity because, although locked up, they will still eventually die. If they die in a negative mode, they will perpetuate negative energy available for future generations to attract.

If you *really* want to help the world, start manifesting that all individuals learn "The Power of Knowing How Life Works". In this way, the world will self-correct.

Groups that Win

For years, cult leaders in many disguises have led people down wrong, disastrous paths of life. Some appeared to be wonderful solutions to life's issues, but egotistical, narcissistic leaders, who promoted euphoric solutions or demon-based doomsday comings, usually fueled them with their own dominant thoughts and the neutral innocence followed them.

Since my November 2009 experience, I have studied cults and various questionable individuals, including those who entranced the German people during World War II, namely Adolf Hitler. I also studied atrocities like Jim Jones' Jonestown massacre in northwestern Guyana at the Peoples Temple and the Waco siege at the Branch Davidian ranch in Texas.

Those who lead these cults were evil and self-serving. We must guard against opportunists who seek to destroy the meaning of "The Knowledge". One very bad or misdirected person can lead a group of people, who are looking for answers or are willing to let outside influences govern their lives into chaos and doom, because they have not set a direction for themselves. We know the results of these kinds of manipulators and their egotistical actions, motivated by power and greed. One of my main concerns while evaluating how to distribute the knowledge was to make sure that I learned how to explain this powerful knowledge in a way that never misled or compelled people to create evil conclusions. No political alignments; no cults; just share "The Knowledge".

The group that overpowers another group with thought wins, which is why Adolf Hitler was powerful in his early years. When the world woke up and started manifesting the fall of Hitler, the universe guided the resolution. That's why political parties win, why sports teams win, and why religious beliefs spread.

Those who consciously attract "their" will against others, such as Jim Jones, Adolf Hitler, Osama Bin Ladin and Muammar Gaddafi, manipulate unsuspecting populations. When the controlled group finally takes control through unified thought, change happens; if no one resists the overpowering person or group, events like Jonestown occur. This pattern occurs throughout history.

For example, one might argue that the early slaves had no choice but to build the pyramids, or had no say about being shipped to America. This was because slave traders' "willpower" focused on obtaining slaves, and slave owners focused on keeping them as slaves. Slave traders were attracting the ability to control humanity for their own greed and profit. The slaves simply were living in neutral and were unwilling victims.

The enslaved never considered being made slaves, so they focused on things like feeding their families and building huts. They did not focus on *not becoming* slaves because they had no knowledge of what a slave was. As soon as the enslaved group focused on what was happening to them, and attracted ways to defend themselves, change began. It took years to implement that change but, if they had not used what we now know as "The Power of Knowing How Life Works," they would not have advanced out of slavery.

You can apply "The Knowledge" to every situation in the world: war, peace, wealth, poverty, winning, losing, success, failure, happiness, and sadness. Think of a topic and apply "The Knowledge" to help you obtain a positive result—that is, *if* you want a positive result!

"The Knowledge" I received wants us to be independent thinkers rather than be led by misdirected, self-serving narcissists. By understanding "The Power of Knowing How Life Works," you can identify attempts for manipulation before damage occurs.

Who or What Is Stronger?

If the environment is stronger than your willingness to think for yourself, then the environment will dominate your decision process. That's why we have gangs, why political parties survive, and why leaders of all kinds have followers. When you don't think for yourself, you will be forced to take a fork in the road, which your environment wishes you to take, unless you have chosen a different path. Only you can make that choice. You and only You!

Follow or lead—*it's up to you*. I choose to distribute this knowledge so I will.

This will easily explain why a child, who is born into a particular environment, has the potential to change their basic beliefs even after being raised by dominating influences. Somewhere along the way—through friends at school, by reading books or just manifesting a positive life—they decide to make their own choices.

The radical militant black man may have some white-man particles which he has attracted out of the universe. The redneck may have particles from a black man who walked the earth hundreds of years ago. Even a child born to a bigot may have attracted particles from a progressive thinker and therefore has the potential to change the way he or she chooses to live, in spite of the environment in which they were born. That is why a country boy, with no environmental support, can end up as an area vice president of sales for a big company and eventually attract "The Knowledge" that has the capacity to change the world! "The Knowledge" is available to everyone, even you!

Take yourself out of the whole "negative awareness arena"—where everything looks terrible, useless, and even hopeless—before stagnation, apathy, and depression set in. Don't let your environment pull you down. Negative people project negative thoughts, so keep them from running and ruining your life.

Mental and Physical Problems

Here's an important note about mental illness: *If you are suffering from true clinical depression, treat it seriously.* "The Knowledge" is not a substitute for obtaining professional assistance. It is imperative that you first get proper help in order to apply the techniques I am sharing with you. Applying "The Knowledge" could speed recovery.

Even though the phenomenon surrounds us, many components are contained within your body parts: cells, atoms, bone, flesh, organs, brain mass. With the intricate workings that must come together during the growth process, there will be flaws—just like the ones in a new car. Fifty cars may be perfect and, of course, you will buy the one with a flaw—especially if you believe you will.

Flaws may exist in the genetic makeup of the brain or cells that cause depression. The neurons or synapses misfire or do not form completely during construction. Flaws are not an individual's fault, so why treat them that way? My nephew has Down Syndrome and we could not love him any more than if he were a pro football player. Those flaws need to be professionally repaired or at a minimum, understood.

Apart from true clinical depression, however, it is possible to overcome the sadness that may surround you by opening yourself to "The Knowledge". If you are sad, "The Knowledge" can help you get happy; if you are already happy, "The Knowledge" can help you get happier; if you fluctuate back and forth between happiness and sadness, congratulations—you are average! However, now you can feel better faster.

Your parents and the psychiatrists of the world believed that your feelings were controllable emotions, and that the base of these feelings came from within you. When you could not execute positive feelings, you blamed yourself.

If you cannot think positively, the answer is not that you have a flaw in your personal makeup. The reality is that you have not realized the source of the refueling. In the simplest terms, the source surrounds you daily, allowing you to either attract or not attract a positive life.

You and only You can make that leap. Attract good things leave the bad.

In contrast, the phenomenon, which was present when the universe began and is present throughout all aspects of life, is the conduit. It surrounds flaws pertaining to disease and contains the mechanism that carries the communication between the cells, which spreads disease. Learn about the space between the cells to understand the communication that is taking place.

My nephew with Down Syndrome feels the love from his family and responds by attracting positive feelings from the universe. He has lived way past others' projections because he likes his life. By utilizing "The Knowledge" along with traditional healing methods, the combination is powerful.

For example, no one attracts cancer into their lives, but if a cell has a defect, which is located within us, it may show up early in life or take many years to develop—60 or 70 earth years, which is a blink of the universal eye. That cell may communicate the defect through the surrounding phenomena to other cells and spread throughout a group of 50 trillion cells located in the human body. It is that communication that holds the key to curing cancer.

Outside influences, which we now call "carcinogens," can also cause damage to cells by blocking their communication mechanisms, cause flaws, and result in the presence of disease. The recipient has no choice but to eliminate the flaws from their body using a variety of methods. This is a very heavy topic, which you should not read haphazardly; for now, you can start to understand that illness is a flaw in the human makeup and communicates through the existing phenomenon.

When Tragedy Strikes

I was ready to send this book to the editor on Mar. 11, 2011, and decided instead to comment on a big news event. A 9.0 earthquake hit Japan and many people lost their lives. First and foremost, our positive thoughts should be focused on the tragedy and all of the people affected. I subsequently waited more than a year to clarify more insights.

The reason I felt compelled to write this section is simple: Now that you possess "The Power of Knowing How Life Works," and I have shared how the universe began, you should be able to analyze this tragedy—and others like it—with a clearer understanding. Our imbalance of thought creates a fluctuation in the vibrations and waves that exist around us and huge natural disasters are the result of that imbalance of thought.

No superior being inflicted His wrath on those innocent Japanese people. The rumblings of the earth happened because the phenomenon, which created the universe and exists even today was in transition. With the constant moving of the waves of the phenomenon, things shift, and that makes the earth move.

Changes in the makeup of earth as we know it, and constant shifts of the phenomenon, will create natural changes in our environment. Doomsday, caused by evil retribution sent from the heavens to make us repent for our sins, is not coming. It does not work that way. However, unless we get back in harmony and balance we will create our own disasters created by our thoughts, feelings and beliefs being out of sync.

As waves move, they are not always consistent. The constant growth of fixed items—mountains, rivers, and ocean floors—causes natural disasters—not some fictitious demon from the depth of a volcano. The phenomenon shifts and grows, and sometimes erupts from the buildup of energy. *That is all.* It is no longer mystical; there is no one to blame, no evil gods or devils. This is a natural progression of the phenomenon.

None of the Japanese people deserved or manifested the tragedy; it just happened. It was a flaw. Expansion or imbalance of the phenomenon in the earth created a disaster. If the projected doomsday ever came, it would not be because of demons in earthquakes; it would be because of a shift in the earth caused by a very active phenomenon, which surrounds all objects including mountains, oceans, and every living thing. No one killed in this tragedy or any other tragedy expected it to happen.

It just did.

People always ask me if a doomsday is possible. If enough people believed it because of the power of our thoughts then yes, we could create our own demise. I know my thoughts are powerful as are yours. So stop thinking bad things and think good things. DAH!

No One Asks for Accidents and War

Accidents may or may not be caused by your environment. For example, a drunk driver, or someone using a cell phone or texting while driving, is not fate; it is carelessness. If this person veers into your lane, it is an accident. If you are the perpetrator, then it is not destiny—it is stupidity. The other party whom you injure did not attract you or the accident; they were just driving along. There is no destiny or predetermined curse of any kind, so don't blame yourself unless, of course, you caused the accidents by careless actions. No one asks to be injured in accidents. Do not constantly fear accidents.

War is perpetrated from hate. Usually, one man's hate spawns more hate, people become subjects of the hate, and war breaks out. If we listen to "The Knowledge," we can avoid this. If we stop following egotistical leaders and make our own correct choices, it will lead to peace and happiness. I have tears in my eyes just thinking about how easy we could achieve peace on this planet if everyone possessed and implemented

"The Power of Knowing How Life Works," with love and compassion vs. hate and anger.

Imagine! (take a minute and Google the words from the John Lennon song; Imagine) Listen to the words and resonate with the song. Imagine that anything is possible.

Take a minute to reflect and gather your thoughts! Remember where you are going to gather them from!

Bergabada and the Law of Attraction

The Quick Answer

As people learned that I was writing a book called "*The Power of Knowing How Life Works,*" they looked at me with impatient stares and wanted "the answer" in less than 20 words.

"Quick! *Give me the answer!* I have to go get a cup of coffee."

"Okay. That's nice, Don, but you have not given me any *specifics* yet and we have been talking for almost *two minutes!*"

I understand why they are in such a hurry. How do I relate to them? It's easy. I was just like them. It was part of my training, so I understand the challenges I face. They have programmed themselves to believe that there is no answer, so why waste their time listening to the biggest piece of information that has ever been disclosed? There is a fourth dimension; thoughts, feelings, beliefs, emotions and knowledge come from the universe not from individual minds; major disease can be controlled if we block the communication between cells to recap just a few.

As I mentioned earlier, it is the first time that I have ever heard anything like this, although I believe that I am not the first person to receive the download nor will I be the last. I understand how egotistical that must sound. Before "The Knowledge" arrived, I would have also looked at anyone who made these kinds of claims in the same way. I am however, very comfortable making the statements because this is not about me. It is about "The Knowledge", which has arrived for you. It is your knowledge to accept or reject.

Traditional Teachings

If you set aside traditional beliefs, you can start to understand "The Knowledge;" however, the existing consciousness community although they seem progressive in thought still cling to traditional teachings. I must acknowledge their beliefs, although their combined traditional beliefs have in fact created the roadblocks to understanding and truly grasping new concepts such as "The Power of Knowing How Life Works."

Some may call the single source from which we originate "God" or the "God particle." If you believe that a superior being, who created the world, caused the first interaction of the phenomena, I respect that. In fact, I will *never* try to dispute it. The beauty of "The Knowledge" is that it is truly universal. It leaves open your personal interpretation of the question, "What *was* that phenomenon that created that first interaction that in turn started the creation of the universe?"

There was no return address on "The Knowledge" when it arrived, so I will not dilute "The Knowledge" with speculation of what source supplied it. Ample speculation exists about that issue spread out over thousands of years. Instead, I invite you to make your own assessments. If this makes sense welcome to my world, it is the way it works.

Of course, you can continue to believe without hesitation that a superior being created the phenomenon; however, I will then ask you the logical follow-up question:

"What created the superior being?" I know, I know that's what makes him or her superior; I got it!

Think out of the box!

The Law of Attraction and the Consciousness Community

The same phenomenon that was present at the beginning of the universe connects all of us today, which is why the Law of Attraction (a metaphysical belief that "like attracts like," that positive and negative thinking bring about positive and negative physical results, respectively) works. People use the concept of the Law of Attraction to describe something, but they don't know how it started.

Other than company-sponsored events, I never attended seminars until after my experience that November morning. Then, I discovered the existing consciousness community and became involved in various ways: attending seminars, following Loral Langemeier "LiveOutLoud" coaching and "Big Table," and joining Bernhard Dohrmann's CEO Space community.

The more I learned, watched, and communicated, the more I discovered the depth of existing awareness to many of the insights that came to me directly from the universe, and the more confused I became about new information versus existing information. Although I have never doubted my download, because it was pure and genuine, I did not learn about this information from others by reading books or tapes, I received "The Knowledge" because I asked for an answer. Then I accepted it as it arrived.

There have been many books outlining the manifestation process and, if you are of a conscious mind, you will know their titles. If you are still searching for answers, you could always take a trip to the self-help section of your local bookstore where you will find multiple choices to investigate. As an alternative, keep reading this series of books.

I hope that my message helps you to understand the source and meaning of the universal laws to which the other books refer. "The Knowledge", as it arrived, gave very clear insights that these writings were a great beginning reference but the existing books stopped short of the true explanation of *why* the universal Law of Attraction works.

My insights will help you understand why it is important to understand how the Law of Attraction works, so you will not be compelled to discount this critical universal law. The consciousness community and their books and CD's provide learning tools and compliment "The Knowledge". They utilize the universal Law of Attraction and spread the word. They have also laid the groundwork for the challenge I face in distributing "The Knowledge," which has been provided to me from the universe, it will arrive to other "ordinary people." the question remains, will they accept the challenge or not?

Although the current self-help community is powerful, billions of people worldwide are still looking for answers; more importantly, some have stopped or have never even started looking. The latter group will not tap into the self-help community for fear of contradicting their traditional teachings. I heard a couple of people refer to the self-help community as a bunch of "tree huggers" and reject the notion that a new world is evolving. They did not need to attend motivational seminars nor did they understand the need for presenting them. These people are stuck in neutral.

I understand, I was one of those people living in neutral for many years while I prepared to receive "The Knowledge" which was delivered to me to help facilitate the process of assimilation of thought between the "get it" and the "just don't care" communities.

Why Doesn't It Work for Everyone?

Most people, when faced with negative issues, cannot easily rid themselves of the negative energy and replace it with positive energy. They harbor negative energy, and positive energy cannot find its path. It sounds good, but it's hard to think positively all the time; however, it is what you *must* do in order to manifest positive things into your life. If you surround yourself in a reality of negative emotions you constantly recycle those emotions through your processor, over and over again because they are readily available, they surround you and you keep them there as your reality. Get rid of it!

Many believe that to obtain abundance in your life, you manifest (that is, ask politely) for what you need and then the universe will provide happiness and abundance. Many people believe in a god or superior being as the source of their manifesting power. They sometimes use a different term; they pray. They have control, they get to choose.

In order for you to acquire "The Knowledge", you must intently focus on what you want and actively walk through the open doors that the universe has provided for you. You cannot just sit on a couch and expect riches to come to you; you will eventually get hungry, have to get up, and refuel yourself. However, now that you know where "The Knowledge" comes from—and more importantly, *why* it works—you can utilize the Law of Attraction, the "attraction of knowledge, thoughts, feelings, beliefs and emotions" and master your thoughts with positive results.

You have been doing the manifestation process (or not) your whole life. For example, imagine wanting to be a bus driver. You open the newspaper and right in front of you, you see an ad for a bus driver. Your heart sinks! You would love to apply for the bus-driving job, but you have never driven a bus before and do not even have a license to drive a bus.

This is a fork in the road. You can easily turn to the next page of the newspaper and discount the job staring you in the face or you can put the paper down, look in the phone directory for bus-driving schools, make the call, get dressed, get the training, and go get the job (or not).

You can easily say that seeing a job listed in the paper means nothing, or you can understand that, because you wanted to be a bus driver, the universe provided the link. Think of the thousands of ads in various newspapers around the country and the fact that you just "happen" to see that one. It is a link like every other occurrence in your life. This link is the phenomenon working, which surrounds everything in the universe. The universe is filled with knowledge and the phenomenon provides the links through particles of thoughts, feelings, beliefs and emotions.

If you continue to sit on the couch, you will eventually attract negative energy into your life, and end up depressed and confused. Whom will you blame? You will blame a book called, *The Secret or some other writing* because you will think it misled you, or you will blame society or you will blame your parents or your 4th grade teacher for keeping you after school. Make some new choices, store your old baggage in "the box" and take action. Remember the universal knowledge cannot distinguish between positive and negative thoughts; therefore, it cannot help you sort out your problems ... *only you can do that.*

Exercise: Imagine you can see the old baggage surrounding you in the form of thoughts or emotions. Visualize them around you, now watch them stay put as you walk away.

Receiving "The Knowledge"

You still may be thinking, "I already *know* that thinking positively and feeling good thoughts are necessary to being happy," and "I *know* I'm the only person who can make changes," but *do you do it?* How is it working so far! Is everything just perfect?

The majority of people will say "no."

(Don't forget: I was in your shoes for 56 years.)

You have traditionally learned how life works from your current environment, past writings, stories, communications, and behavioral paradigms and dogma passed down through the ages and from actual history. You have learned from reading, studying, listening, analyzing, and reviewing scientific principles of quantum energy and physics. Then you formulated, calculated, and drew conclusions from that existing knowledge to keep evolving as a society. Are you still in neutral, same thing every day, make changes.

Some people meditate for years, trying to find their life purpose or bliss, or whatever else they want. They search for their "soul," or try to expand their minds to feel one with the universe. Others trek to far-off mountains or peaceful retreats as they desperately try to achieve an ever-elusive state of inner consciousness.

These focused thinkers want to achieve something that no one else is able to achieve. They want to gather up a powerful chill, they want to fulfill a traditional spiritual need, a euphoric feeling of accomplishment, or an inner peace that no one else is able to fulfill.

They are all looking in the wrong places! The answer surrounds them daily.

You can find it all just by simply be aware of the particle soup that we live in.

Now you have something you never had before: "The Power of Knowing How Life Works."

The Power of Knowing How Life Works teaches that "The Knowledge" exists and is accessible to you. Anything is possible if you focus on your needs. I was never able to meditate to any significant result; however, I have been able to manifest results my entire life, and that is where our learning begins. Look at your own life and understand why you made specific choices along the way then determine that you can now make new choices.

Surrounding yourself with "The Knowledge" and achieving the feeling of the presence of the universe surrounding you is actually very simple. "The Knowledge" is already "there." It surrounds you. You can feel confident that the answers and the keys to all of the doors, through which you will need to walk on your life's path, are contained in that surrounding feeling of the phenomenon, which contains "The Knowledge" from which you can draw the answers to which I am referring.

Try it. If your response is that you pray, and that God is walking with you, then you should know by now that I am okay with that answer. Being surrounded by "The Knowledge" should be an empowering experience. Having "The Knowledge" from the universe delivered to us is the source of that power.

Questions and Answers

I have learned to ask the universe a specific question regarding the item that has surfaced. Then I attract the answer to that question. I believe the confirmation when it arrives—whether by an individual who comes into my life or by some occurrence.

I then manifest the "affirmation" of the answer relating to the question. Then I affirm the answer by asking the following question, "How is it working so far?"

Here are some examples:

- **"We already have social welfare programs in place to feed the starving children in America. Why still worry about it?"**

Affirmation question: How is it working so far?

Answer: It's not! We still have hungry kids.

- **"We have unemployment insurance. Why still worry about jobs being lost in America?"**

Affirmation question: How is it working so far?

Answer: It's not! Our tax base is eroding, our infrastructure is collapsing, and our schools are crumbling around us. There is no dignity in collecting unemployment.

- **"Ask yourself, is the person who just entered my life a person whom I attracted? Did they attract me into their lives, or is it just a neutral occurrence?"**

Affirmation question: How is it working so far? (the interaction)

Answer: This interaction will add (or not add) value based on the need in one of our lives. Either they needed me or I needed them at that moment in time. It works for every interaction: I need either input from someone or some service or just a smile from a friend. Maybe they needed me, it really does not matter as long as the connection is made and acknowledged by you.

"The Knowledge" and Modern Society

"The Knowledge" applies to modern society in the same context that it has applied for thousands of years. It is critical that we also answer the question so often asked in today's world: "What's in it for me?"

Here are just a few examples of how this applies to you and your family:

- **"Your kids are out of control."**

If your kids can read this book and understand that, as early as the age of 10, I started manifesting my future and it worked, then maybe, when they sit by themselves under the stars, they will at least try to manifest a good life for themselves by drawing from the universal consciousness. When they say, "I tried that, but it is *still* not working," remind them that it took me 57 years before I was able to look back through my life and manifest "The Knowledge," which showed me "how it all worked." The key point is that it worked for everything I did throughout my life instantaneously from an early age; it just took me 57 years and a powerful download of knowledge and insights to understand it.

- **"You are going through a divorce and you don't understand why."**

I have been happily married for 39 years to the same beautiful partner. The reason is simple: I wanted to be married, even with the ups and downs that life tosses at us—kids, stress, and money issues—and all the highs, lows, and challenges that life presents daily, I always wanted to stay married to my wife.

I manifested her into my life in the beginning. (Remember the white house in that small country town?) As challenges popped up throughout our lives, I always manifested us staying together and working out our issues. Now I understand how it worked. If I had manifested the thought, "I want out," the universe, not understanding anything but my intentions would have supplied thoughts, feelings, and beliefs that would have over time pushed us apart. This is not rocket science. If one partner is not getting what they need—sexually, emotionally, spiritually, or whatever—and starts to manifest a different solution, the universe cannot differentiate right from wrong and makes the adjustments that you or your significant other manifest. That's how other people come into relationships; they fill a need or a void. Plus, they arrive with their own needs and therefore the hook-up is facilitated.

We are all connected by the phenomenon so, when a person is in the universe and manifesting a relationship, and their energy matches up with another person in the universe looking for a similar relationship, then the universe has an easy job.

If you say, "I do not want a divorce," but a divorce takes place, someone in the partnership was manifesting change. It may have been *you*, just by your unhappy thoughts, which contained potentially negative results.

It is heavy stuff, but you can still apply "The Knowledge" to it. *You and only you* can make changes in your life. In a relationship, there are two people who manifest an end result, even if it's done quietly by their own thoughts. If one person manifests a separation or divorce, and it comes about, then that partner that is leaving was manifesting their lives with more focus and resolve. The other partner is left to wonder why.

They may have been in neutral and as explained the dominant thoughts win out.

My wife never had a chance! She is stuck with me because of the power I personally had to manifest my life—unless, of course, I get complacent and she is manifesting a different outcome. It works for everyone, and I have no corner on that market. If she decides to leave, I'm going with her!

- **"You declare; I can't stand my job. I want to leave but I cannot afford to do so."**

If you go to work every day, hate the people for whom you work, or are mistreated by that company, and everyone in the company feels the same way; the company will not make its goals and will eventually perish in the inferno of negative energy. The end result is that you are out of your job.

The universe will make adjustments; however, the converse is also true. If you believe in your company and their goals, and they have a sincere interest in giving back to society and taking care of your family, and you are manifesting great things for the business, and you and your co-workers all feel the same way and are all manifesting positive results, you will help the company thrive and grow. It really is that simple. Doom and gloom thoughts result in doom and gloom results; positive energy results in a positive life. I watched a major corporation affirm this insight as they went from a major power in their industry to nothing more than a place to go to work and eventual bankruptcy.

An Explosion of Knowledge

The Power of Knowing How Life Works is not just a book or an attempt to create thought. It is a road map to your future, and your future is exciting, dynamic, and fantastic! An explosion of knowledge will be manifested from the universe as humanity realizes its power. As our collective, progressive knowledge has increased in the universe, the more progressive knowledge is available for everyone to attract. This knowledge is the basis of our abundance, happiness, and cooperation—not competition—for those who understand what it means.

Dec. 21, 2012—the end of the Mayan calendar—will come and go. There will be a change in how we exist, but it will not be a doomsday change. It will be a *fantastic* change. The Mayan calendar will not end because it is the end of the world; instead, it is the beginning of new hope and happiness. The Mayan people were part of humanity, and humanity developed the calendar. It has nothing to do with doomsday but instead with limited thinking on their part. (I send my apologies to any Mayans who may still be supplying us with knowledge, which they deposited into the universe when they died. It's just a calendar!) The Mayan people may very well have believed that if we did not have it all figured out by the December 2012 date that the world would have already come to an end and we were doomed, but that is not so. The end of the calendar is not a pre-determination of some oncoming doom. What if they just got tired of working on the calendar? Maybe their lives ended before they could continue, if they were thinking doom and gloom they may have manifested it on themselves through the power of thought........think good things; it makes a difference to all of us!

I suggest you plan your parties because, on that day, if you choose to make it happen, your life will change with an amazing transformation toward a positive spirit and with the unity of humanity based on understanding "The Power of Knowing How Life Works." Or if you wish, you can start today – it's your choice!

The Power of
Positive Choices

"Passing on" with Your Energy Particles

If you spend your life with positive thoughts and positive feelings, and surround yourself with positive energy, then, when you "pass on," that positive energy is dispersed into the universe. The opposite is also true. If you pass on from your physical being surrounded by negative energy, and end your life with negative thoughts and negative feelings, then—you guessed it—you spend eternity as negative energy, which will infect generations to come.

My insights revealed that you must look not only inside for your answers but also outside your physical body, and live your life as you will want to live it for eternity. I am hoping that, when I say "inside," you now understand that it includes the powerful phenomenon filled with knowledge, which surrounds you and every part of your body.

It is *up to you* to attract the positive or negative energy into your life as you move through the universe. It's out there and you walk through it every day, attracting different particles into your life. It surrounds you and every square inch of your body and being.

Reap What You Sow

When your environmental support team (e.g., parents, grandparents, authors, educators, and philosophers) told you to think positively, they were 100% correct. You are surrounded by the phenomenon we have labeled "energy," now you know they are particles; so why not gather them up and utilize it to improve and support your life?

You are the one who attracts the type of energy from the universe that you have identified. *You are the one* who makes the choice about which type of energy—positive or negative—to attract. Along with it comes your ability to attract knowledge that is stored within the phenomenon. These particles deposited there by past generations in the form of thought particles are there for you to utilize.

Your parents just "knew" that it made sense to think positively. I am now confirming that you have the ability and "The Knowledge" to apply those teachings because *they are true.* The key is to make sure that you attract and utilize it from the true source of "The Knowledge."

An old term, which the nonfarm kids may not understand, is "You reap what you sow"; in other words, "you get out what you put in." The funny thing about these outdated sayings is that they are true, but nobody knew why.

Here's the new version: "What you attract from the universe is what you will exhibit as your life and your reality." Don Saunders

We are tied together by a common thread that began the universe—the phenomenon. Because of that relationship, "you" are the phenomenon, as is everything else, so when you attract from the universe it becomes your reality, and your reality in turn attracts from the universe similar results. However, you can change your reality anytime you wish simply by manifesting new thoughts.

However, if you want to change your life, you "must" attract a different result from the universe. If you are happy with your life, then you will in turn attract results that compliment how you live. I realize now that thinking positive thoughts and attracting positive energy have been the reason why I was so successful in manifesting whatever I was seeking.

The opposite is also true: Don't "plant" negative thoughts or feelings into your thought process. The universe is supplying the particles of thought; it cannot sort out thoughts for you. "Reject" negative-thinking behaviors or you'll get the sinister payback: You will reap what you have sown, which, of course, would be negative results because you focused on negative energy. Think positively because the universe only hears your request, and you confuse the request when adding the negative thoughts and feelings into the mix. Caution: "Don't ask for what you don't want; ask only for what you want"

Thoughts create feelings, which create behaviors, which create actions.

Can We Heal Ourselves?

If our cells are damaged, we must go into the proverbial garage for repair. Think through the whole process of how life works. Knowing that the phenomenon, which created us, surrounds the cells, we have the ability to attract positive thoughts from that acquired knowledge—the "universal knowledge base"—that exists in the universe.

Thoughts, feelings, beliefs, emotions and knowledge are part of the universe. The phenomenon stores the knowledge and surrounds everything, so manifesting positive results is the same as manifesting good health through manifesting positive feelings. If you are sick, attracting positive energy will help you heal faster and help the doctors cure you more quickly because that phenomenon, which surrounds each cell, is a communication device with each cell and organ in your body. The water in each cell has memory so grab all of the positive particles that pass through your body and retain them.

"The Power of Knowing How Life Works" will not heal you on its own any more than if you wished that your car did not have a big dent; however, if you think positively that you can get everything fixed and then do something about it, you have a powerful combination. Damaged parts need to be replaced or repaired do not ignore this fact.

In all fairness, sometimes flaws have gone undetected for so long that you cannot repair them. That is still no excuse for giving up because, as you learn how the whole thing works, you will understand that a positive end equates to eternal positive energy. You can supply the universe with good stuff to refuel itself, even in your last days of physical life, by thinking positively. Celebrate life and create great particles for all to use.

Positive Awareness

It is up to you to learn to "accept" and look for positive thoughts—and even create them if need be. Put yourself in a state of positive awareness where everything looks good or at least seems hopeful. This one tiny action can cause enormous positive changes, positive feelings, and forward movement, and will attract positive people and positive situations into your life. If you do this—even part of the time—you will begin to realize just how simple it is to live in harmony, joyfully, abundantly, and without apology.

Accept positive energy into your life. Positive energy is tremendously more powerful than negative energy unless you allow negative energy to take over. The positive energy in the universe will open doors that you would not have believed could ever have been opened for you.

"So, why should we believe "The Knowledge", Don?"

You don't have to. Just look at the television news or read the paper.

How is it working so far?

If thinking positively and feeling good feelings all the time are well-known practices, then why do we have fights, disagreements, negativity, sadness, depression, and devastation caused by wars, crime, and mayhem?

As Bob Dylan once insightfully wrote, "The answer is blowin' in the wind."

Round and Round

Although parents, grandparents, numerous authors, educators, and philosophers told you to "think positively," you still have not adapted it fully into your life. My own family struggles with this issue, and our discussions, which go round and round, help me understand that the majority of the world has the same questions:

"How are we supposed to think positively all the time? How are we supposed to *do* that?" Life throws curve balls and curve balls are tough to hit. But you can hit them.

How you believe is how you leave and how you are available to return.

Positive and negative energy, which is stored in the phenomenon that surrounds us, is available to you. You have the ability to feel good or bad based on what type of particles you have withdrawn from the universe. *It is up to you!*

I strive to embrace positive thoughts and concentrate on good feelings every minute of my life and not be concerned with the source. My life—before and after Tuesday, Nov. 17, 2009—is significantly different. My physical being looks the same, ok, I'm older; but I assure you that I am two different individuals. "The Knowledge" I manifested that morning changed my life forever. If you listen, ponder, remain focused and believe in the possibilities; your life will also change in a very good way.

My Early "Why" Questions

In my early years as I was growing up, I was confused by the concept of "destiny." I was told that destiny (or "fate" or "chance") marked out in advance the main road map for life; however, no explanation ever made sense because no one could explain how destiny worked. The most common response I heard was, "God has a master plan for you."

I added this "master plan" concept to my list of other "why" questions about life:

- Why do people believe in destiny?
- Why did that happen to him and not to me?
- Why are they rich and I am not?
- Why do professional athletes have excessive sports-related talents?

I began to ask my question: How does this thing we call life actually work?

Slipping and Recovering

I occasionally find myself slipping back into negative thoughts. I still have traditionally learned behaviors and environmental factors surrounding me because they exist in the universal consciousness, the same ones that existed through the first 56 years of my life, which I stumble through day by day. The major difference is that now, I immediately start the recovery process back into thinking positive thoughts and attracting positive energy. My recovery time is much quicker because of "The Knowledge" I gained. *That's the real power ... and it's free.* Your old thoughts are always going to be available.

You know that your life can change in a nanosecond, but few ever think it will happen to them. I had no wild, remote thoughts of having this knowledge delivered to me. However, I am certainly thankful that it came my way.

The key ingredient to the manifestation process is to be willing to accept "The Knowledge" or the answer when it arrives. When a tragic event occurs, we always wonder, "Why?" If it is a tragic change that affects you personally, we ask, "Why me?"

These are no longer questions in my life; in fact, and strangely enough, I never questioned "why" this experienced happened "to me". I knew the answer from the insights that came along with "The Knowledge". I was able to manifest and was willing to accept it when it arrived because my insights provided me with the explanations, and affirmed that I had been training for "The Knowledge" to arrive in order to distribute it to you. You will get your answers because our source is the same, your focus, your belief and your ability to accept and understand the answers as the particles arrive will be the key to your success.

What Controls Your Actions?

Numerous authors refer to the Law of Attraction as either a conscious or a subconscious attraction. You can think of it that way, if you must; however, I now ask you to consider another "out of the box" thought: There are no subconscious thoughts because the phenomenon—"The Knowledge" and energy you receive, which surrounds you—controls your actions. The particles all penetrate throughout your body and because you did not consciously ask for them you mistakenly believe them to be the subconscious.

For those who have spent years studying psychology and psychiatry, please humor me. (I've heard that Sigmund Freud was considered crazy at first, too!) While your ability to attract is not based on conscious or subconscious attraction, you *do* have the power of choice in your life. If you are measuring anything in the human brain you are measuring storage capacity referred to as memory, not creative capacity. Creativity comes from outside the brain directly from the universe. Now, the capacity of the brain to process and store will fit along our traditional knowledge as to how the brain functions biologically. Any recall memory that we measure is strictly the measure of storage capacity. When we start to lose that capacity we start to lose our memory. Drink lots of structured water. Water has memory; learn from the fish as they move in schools.

A Fork in the Road

I've always liked the famous saying by Yogi Berra, one of the great orators of our time (okay, he was a baseball catcher for the New York Yankees): "If you come to a fork in the road, take it." He may not have known it at the time, but he was smarter than the people around him who laughed at his Yogi-ism.

His statement was profound. We all come to forks in the road where we have to make major—and possibly life-changing—decisions. When you come to one of those "forks in the road," you must make the choices for your life. No one can tell you which fork to take. Others may try to make those choices for you, but even if Yogi didn't consciously state it, you decide which fork to take when you come to it. It is up to you to determine the outcome of your life. *You and only you* make the choices. The last choice someone should have made for you was that last second before your conception.

Forks are not just for every major decision. You make decisions every minute of every day of your life, all of which affect your path. For example: Are the following occurrences' destiny or free will? Before you even read you should have this all figured out. If you have chosen free will you are ready for all of the other books coming in the series of "The Power of Knowing How Life Works".

- What makes you pick up a glass of water and drink it rather than just move it to a new location on the counter? Destiny or free will?
- What makes your fingers move when you hold them in front of your face?
- What makes your feet move one step at a time as you move around freely?

Here is the great news: You can come to forks, at numerous times and at any age, and *it is never too late to choose the right fork.* In fact, if you really break it down, every decision you make is a fork in the road, which means that you have total control over your life. The only right or wrong fork is the one that resonates with you but try to make good choices so that you can have a happy, healthy and vibrant life for all of us to enjoy.

Step Back and Think

It's audience participation time! Here's what I'd like you to do:

- Put the book down and get a piece of paper.
- Step back from your normal thought processes and think about how you have lived your life so far. Everything, the good, the bad, the ugly.
- Write down the number of times you came to a major fork in the road.
- When you were at each of these forks, carefully examine what drove your decision to go right instead of left, or left instead of right. Do I get married or not?
- Think about how many times *you* made the choice of which fork to take versus how many times you just took a certain fork because the surrounding circumstances in your life said to turn left, so you turned left.

You exist in the phenomenon that surrounds you. How you think and move are direct results of the process of how life works. As you examine your list, you may realize that you stopped at a fork in the road and stared at a caution sign because you really didn't know which way to go. Take action, make a decision and move forward.

At other times, perhaps you were like the majority of people who do not choose any fork at all and just stand still. Maybe you waited for someone or something else in your environment to make a decision for you. If that was the case, you might as well have sent up a red flag because decisions made for you by other people will be the result of "their will" trying to adjust your life to meet "their" needs.

How many times have you listened to others because it seemed "logical" or "safe"? Don't let your environment, another person, your fear, or some other situation make decisions for you and then blindly go along wherever their decision takes you. If you do, you may never find the true answers about your life, and you will have no one to blame but yourself. The political, corporate and religious leaders of the world have learned how to have you serve them for "their" motives. Make your own choices!

The universe wants you to discover the phenomenon. Starting right now, feel the presence of the universe surrounding you in every activity of your life—*everything!*

If you accept the concept that the phenomenon, which surrounds you daily, is the same source for the world's knowledge, and that you have access to that source (and to the information and attraction–power contained within it), then you can utilize "The Knowledge" to create a new direction for yourself or whatever else you want.

The phenomenon is the unidentified thread that connects all things in our universe and links us. Therefore, if you need people to assist you in a project, focus on the need—not specifically on the individual—and the universe will send people to you. Someone may come along who does not seem to fit your need, but do not discount them; you never know about their connections (through the phenomenon) they may "link" you to the person you really do need to meet. The more you stay focused and positive, the greater the chance that people will show up with their special gifts or contributions to help fulfill your need. Sometimes these people provide knowledge of what to do; sometimes they provide guidance of what "not" to do. It is all part of the knowledge being provided by the universe. It is massive knowledge; it is all of "The Knowledge" of the world.

When you stay focused on the need and you believe in a great result, you will draw from the universe "The Knowledge" of how to accomplish what you want to accomplish. You won't need tools or visuals because you will know when you have accomplished the exercise ... it will be finished!

Choose the Right Fork

The phenomenon, which surrounds you, supplies the source for your decisions, but you must choose the right fork. There is a reason they call it *your* life. Only you can decide which fork to take to determine your path in life. You are like a magnet that is capable of attracting the particles you need into your body and surroundings. You choose your own type of energy (for lack of a better earthly word), that you will use to live within your physical being. Stop supporting the self-serving leaders and wall street greed mongers.

"Don, we've heard the 'think positive thoughts' and 'feel positive feelings' pitches our whole lives. We cannot *possibly* think and feel that way *all the time!*"

Yes, you have heard it before, but do you know *why* it has been taught? Do you know the real answer to *why* it is important? If not, please read on.

How you choose to live your life determines how you continue in the cycle of eternity. Do you want to attract positive or negative energy? It really is that simple. You can request a boost of positive energy or focus on a particular thought powerful enough to attract "The Knowledge" into your life. If you want to attract positive energy, you will lead a life that supports that end; if you are complacent or want to attract negative energy, your life will take a negative twist.

A major question is HOW; how are we going to manifest positive energy instead of negative energy. Answer: It has to do with all of the earthly words that you are already familiar with, intent, focus, belief, hope and understanding. When the particles that surround us and permeate us every Nano-second of our lives they basically reside around you unsolicited in many cases. You walk through the particle soup and the particles simply mingle with your existing reality which also surrounds you. As the particles penetrate your reality only you get to determine the outcome of the interaction.

All of your cells are composed of water, water has memory and therefore can either retain or reject the interaction of the particles that are processed or that pass through your reality. How we know which ones to choose is yet another question. The complex answer is that the vibrations for our thoughts align with the vibrations in our current reality that we started to develop at conception. The particles that surrounds us are not measurable and exist in great volume around us and as we pass through our environment the particles that resonate with our existing reality are the ones that we retain in memory.

The Test of Saving a Life

I might have saved a man's life on my wife's birthday in 2009, shortly after my November 17th 2009 experience. Maybe he would have been okay. Someone may have found him and returned him to safety. It does not matter. It was a test for me to see if I deeply and passionately understood the insights that I have been given. Driven by love and compassion for others rather than greed and profit.

Here's the story: I went for my normal exercise. After that, I had an idea to go out and get some Christmas gift cards for the people at the spa to thank them for their assistance throughout the year. I also needed a cord for my iPod at Radio Shack and a birthday card from the new card shop for my wife. A normal to do list trip.

On my way back home, I saw an older man stumble and fall in the desert. I slowed down and took a good look at him. I was very aware that he needed help—*my help*. I reached for my phone and realized that I had left it at home in the charger.

Not knowing who he was, or what he was doing there, I decided to get the professionals. He looked like he was wearing pajamas; later, we found out that he was. I turned my van around and looked for a police car, knowing that they are thick as flies in our town. This is usually a great thing except, that day, I found no one to help.

I felt an overwhelming urge to help this man—a stranger— because of something I had pondered the night before relating to one of my insights: Not everyone wants or needs help, so how do I determine who I am supposed to help with "The Knowledge" that I was provided? New to "The Knowledge" I did not have a clear road map.

I stopped at the local fire station and a nice young man came to the door. I told him the story of the man in the desert and asked if he would mind calling the police for me as I had forgotten my cell phone. I said that I would wait in front of the fire station. Seconds later, he came back out to tell me that a team of firefighters was going to follow me and see if they could help.

At first, when I saw the men loading into the big fire engine, I said to myself, "Oh, boy! You've done it this time! If this is a false alarm, or if some poor old guy was just walking to 7-11, I am going to feel bad that I bothered these guys."

They came out of the fire station with the yellow fire-truck lights flashing—the whole picture—and I pulled out. They followed me, and my fear of being foolish was overcome by the fact that I was doing the right thing. I knew in my heart that the man needed my help. *I just knew.* I had marked the place where I saw him with a sign on the side of the road and, when we got there, we pulled off the road; however, there was nobody around—no man in pajamas, *nobody.*

I walked back to the truck. One of our local heroes, who had listened to and followed me, came out of the truck and explained very professionally that there are many homeless people in the area. If they combed the desert for all of the people wandering around, they would be unavailable to help others. I told him that I understood and shook his hand. He got back in his big yellow truck, went up to the next intersection, and turned the truck around, going about two miles down the road toward the firehouse.

I continued on my route back home and came around a small curve. *There was the same old man in his pajamas!* He was frail, looked cold and his nose was running, and he seemed disoriented. This time, he was walking down the middle of the road, which had a speed limit of 55 mph. Cars were flying by, blowing horns and nobody stopped.

I pulled up to him and asked if he needed help. He waved me away, but I was able to convince and help him to get off the road. I *knew* he needed help, so—you guessed it—I went up to the next intersection, turned around, and pursued the fire truck once more. I caught them just as they were getting back to the firehouse.

"Guys, something is not right. He is not homeless. I know he is confused and lost. There is an extended care facility about a mile from where I saw him, and I am concerned that he wandered off."

They turned the fire truck around and followed me—again, *nothing*. The young men in the truck had to be thinking that I had lost it or was playing some sort of unfunny game with them. I stood beside the road and thought, "I know he is around here." Maybe he had fallen in the desert; however, I could not ask them to spend more time looking. I know now, because of the force that placed me there, that if I had left at that moment, I would have turned around, gone back, and walked the desert looking for him. I was that convinced that he needed help.

The big yellow fire truck did not turn around this time. They drove around the next curve, escorted by a police car that had joined us, and there he was—a frail, elderly man, his nose running, frozen with thinning hair, and walking along the road in his pajamas!

The firefighters and police officer stopped to help. I got out of my car just long enough to hear him say that he had walked from Pahrump, some 50 miles away. At that point, the firefighters knew he belonged to the extended care facility down the road.

Knowing that I had done the right thing, I left quietly without giving my name because I knew he was now safe. My purpose had not been to receive recognition but rather to help someone. They would take him home and make sure that some family did not have to spend Christmas wondering what had happened to their dad or grandfather. I was overwhelmed with a great feeling that I had helped a man who needed my help.

My insight was affirmed: "Help people who have not yet figured out how to help themselves".

Your Environment Creates the Resonance

While the thought particles that you attract comes from the surrounding universe, your environment creates the tone or resonance for your decision, which refers to the outside influences that affect your daily choices and the decisions you make about your life. You may make a conscious decision, but influences from your environment still affect you.

Friends, family, teachers, the weather, and fear—everything that has influenced your path along the way—are part of your environment. Any one of these factors can change the course of your life; that is, *if* you let your environment influence your decisions too much. Look at everything and everyone as knowledge and choose wisely.

Your environment can influence what type of energy you attract by influencing *you*. If you are born black, you will probably migrate to blacks; if you are born Republican, you will probably carry on those beliefs. If you grew up on a farm and learned how to drive heavy equipment when you were young, as an adult you will most likely look for a job on a farm or in construction. Perhaps you learned how to sew dresses when you were young, so it would come as no surprise that you would look for a job within the garment industry when you grew up. If you spent time in the kitchen watching your mom or grandmother it is no surprise when you end up in the food industry.

"Okay, Don. If that is true—if we carry beliefs from our environmental influences—then how can you say that we are surrounded by knowledge that will allow us to make our own choices?"

"The Knowledge," is always part of you; you and only you have the ability to compile the particles to create your reality. When you choose not to think for yourself, you allow your environment to influence you, and you accept the path others choose for you. I've heard hundreds of people say that they have no plan or expectations about how their lives will turn out. They simply allow their environments to choose their paths. They look in the newspaper for a job, go on an interview, and take the job because it pays money. These people are in neutral, "not that there is anything wrong with that"

Many people are in their current situation because of the environmental conditions under which they grew up or because of someone else's influence over their thought processes at some point. For example, your parents wanted you to go to college, but you wanted to open your own business. You wanted to study drama, but your teachers pushed you into math and science. Now you are stuck working for a big corporation instead of starring on Broadway. By the time you were 30 years old, society had indicated that it was time for you to get married, but you weren't sure you wanted to get married and you walk around tormented about your life instead of focusing on what you really want. You wanted to travel the world, but your parents said, "Get a job!" ... and so it goes. Think about it, had you taken the initiative, known how it worked, you could have been anything you wanted to be. Great news, for the most part, you still can!

Passing It Down

Examine your life:

- Do you follow a political platform because you have completely investigated the politicians' values, or because that is what some outside source, such as your family or friends, taught you?
- In your religious beliefs, did you talk to the source yourself, or just assume that whoever wrote the Bible, the Torah, the Book of Mormon or the Koran wrote it verbatim directly from the source?
- Are the sacred writings that you follow based on eyewitness accounts and discussions, or on an author's interpretation of what they had heard, which may have been passed down through many lips before being captured on paper?

Many of the old, traditional sayings and beliefs already contain pieces of "The Knowledge" because other people have been given this knowledge over hundreds of years or more importantly have access to it directly from the universe. We will continue to receive "The Knowledge" until we get it right! If we don't get it right in one generation, those people will eventually die and "The Knowledge" will be available for the next group to ponder and utilize.

Choosing Your Occupation

- Why is the world so diverse in talent?
- Why do so many different people have so many diverse occupations?

- Why do we have professional athletes, musicians, construction workers, and teachers?

Most traditional thinkers will say that it was a superior being's plan for us. Although I promised not to intrude on your traditional values, I must tell you that we missed that explanation along the way. "The Power of Knowing How Life Works" will give you the answer to ponder. Another option to help sort out the confusion of life.

Pick any occupation: doctor, lawyer, football player, trumpet player, or roofer. If you talk to them, you will see a strong pattern of how it worked:

- The doctor wanted to be a doctor so much that he spent 12 additional years of education attracting knowledge, and his dedication, belief and "focus" on attracting knowledge helped him achieve his goal.
- The lawyer attracted knowledge from past lawyers of the world.
- The musician attracted knowledge on how to play his instrument.

In the case of a roofer, construction worker, or office worker, at first glance you might say that no one grows up wanting to be a roofer. It's not so. The environment may have influenced their thought process, but the roofer *chose* to be a roofer and the man driving a truck *chose* to be a truck driver. "The Knowledge" that was available from the universe that surrounded them created the path for them to follow.

When a person claims that they had no choice in their existing role in the world, it would mean that they are under the watchful eye of a prison guard, but even the prisoner had a choice not to commit the crime.

Use your new knowledge to change your life and the world for the better. How will you make sure that "The Knowledge" stays pure? You will share it with the caveats and warnings that came with my insights. Encourage people to maintain their traditional values until they are comfortable because "The Knowledge" is true. Eventually, people will adapt it as fact and no one will need to challenge it because it challenges no one.

Skeptics

This book was not written with any preconceived notion that you, or anyone else in the world, will fully grasp it. I accept that, however, maybe I can get you to start thinking outside of the proverbial box, at least for a short while.

Good friends—and perfect strangers—have pondered my experience on Nov. 17, 2009, and that is why the knowledge arrived. I have written about many topics in this book that are easy for me to understand (because it happened to me) but are difficult to translate. "The Knowledge" came through an ordinary guy for ordinary people to ponder.

I read every day, hoping to find someone else who had my experience. I am finding hundreds of people who are "enlightened"—those who have been through near-death experiences or who are mediums or channels—and I wish to take nothing from them. "The Knowledge" confirms that "all" is possible; however, after analyzing the videos, books, and lectures, which I have encountered on my journey after that morning, not one so far has had my total "universal experience." Many understand the overall experience, but no one else has lived it; at least not exactly.

I (alone) will know when I encounter that person. This is not an egotistical statement. As I've mentioned, I truly believe that multiple sources have received the information, but they may not have surfaced just yet. (Come to think of it, neither have I—at least not to the extent I will have when this book is published!)

I fully understand the skeptics. My concern is that they do not understand how life works themselves. Therefore, they shut out the possibilities that exist and perpetuate the continued confusion. I would have been skeptical myself had this profound experience not happened to me. The skeptics affect the world the same way as the conscious; through thought. Their confusion adds to the imbalance of the universal consciousness.

My years of deep, personal reflection and powerful life lessons, interwoven with my life experiences, allow me to continually receive insights that further explain more about "The Knowledge," I received. I know where to get "The Knowledge," and this is what I intend to teach you. Knowing that particles contain "The Knowledge" and my insights as to how to distribute this information is what will keep me on course.

Whether you believe me is not important. I will dedicate the rest of my life to the distribution of "The Knowledge" because I know it will change the world. I'm not on an ego trip, nor do I have the desire to be anyone's guru. I just happen to be in possession of a broad understanding, as well as powerful insights, based on an extraordinary experience, and it is my job to deliver "The Knowledge" to you.

Perhaps as you read my story you will be moved to share "The Knowledge" with others. With or without me, "The Knowledge" and the phenomenon that you have read about contains "The Knowledge," it exist. Even if it takes a couple hundred years or more, people will eventually "get it". "The

Knowledge" surrounds us, and it is available to manifest at any time. I understand that I am simply a catalyst for the future explosion of "The Knowledge".

No Followers Please

Currently I own a few retail stores in Lake Las Vegas, Nevada. One morning, a couple came into one of my stores and asked me what my book was called. When I told them, it started a conversation. They both declared that they were Christian.

"Good! Just the people I was waiting for. *Let's talk!*"

They explained that the Bible had too many coincidences tied together by different authors to be anything but authentic and they were devoted in their dedication to God. We had a very nice, always positive, conversation, which lasted almost 45 minutes. I thanked them and assured them that I supported their beliefs, and went back to my writing. Of course it makes sense the words created by knowledge came from the same source that I am discussing in this book.

I have also talked to Catholics, Jews, Muslims, Scientologists, Mormons, Buddhist and Protestants, all of whom have their own strong traditional beliefs. If traditional thinkers believe that God talked to me, then who am I to steal their beliefs from them? From my discussions with this diverse group of people, I know that my future should prove to be very interesting!

It is entirely possible that God, should He exist, has delivered multiple—maybe hundreds, maybe thousands—of messages to different sources and throughout hundreds of years. People say he sent his son, Jesus, to guide us, but the world is divided by religion, language, and conflicts, so what did we learn?

I believe Jesus delivered a message; but as I mentioned toward the beginning of the book, whether or not "The Knowledge" I received was from his father or from the universe is subject to each person's interpretation. I will also state that if a superior being *did* deliver the message to me, he was very intent on making sure it was universal. I truly believe that "The Knowledge" was meant to bring us together utilizing love and compassion, not divide us by our beliefs as many of the world's religions appear to have done over the centuries. How can you kill in the name of your GOD, come on people.

It would be great if we stopped challenging one another, stopped having to be "right" all the time, and started caring about each other. Imagine how powerful the world would be if we felt connected in a way that led to world peace! Why is it that Democrats fight Republicans on everything and the World's Religions fight wars to prove their points? Why do politicians all have money and live lavishly while the slaves follow them? Why do corporations serve the needs of the shareholders before those of the workers? Why do families crumble because of lack of abundance when there is enough for everyone to thrive? Why are we so confused and segmented that we cannot unite"

Religion, politics and prejudice have divided the world. If I do nothing else other than start to unite the world by understanding "The Power of Knowing How Life Works" and how our relationships to everything make up the whole phenomenon, then when I die I will disperse in peace. Someone will manifest my particles and I will have eternal light.

"The Knowledge", if shared appropriately, without greed or profit motives and without the stereotypes and prejudice of today's world, can give us unity and peace. The universe delivered "The Knowledge" through me for you, so we could get back on the track of discovering where "The Knowledge" resides and how to use it for humanity.

Affirmations arrive daily confirming that what happened to me was real. I asked for affirmations to help me start understanding the insights, and they started attracting to me like a magnet, coming from all directions. They came in the form of input from friends, strangers, books, movies, and television—from *all* the things that had already been done. Now I realize that I attract people, things, and situations into my life for a reason: We are all connected from the original phenomenon that created the universe.

Religious Choices

If you receive positive feelings from your traditional beliefs, then please stay with them; however, if you feel that you have your traditional beliefs all sorted out and have formed your overall picture, but still have some gaps or confusion, then open up your mind and think out of the box just a little.

Examine the possibility that *you and only you* have total control over what happens in your life and what you believe. Be willing to accept the possibilities as I show you what the universe wants you to know. Then you can evaluate the validity of the information the universe provided through me and compare it with your traditional thoughts.

If you understand that there is an unknown phenomenon— not because it does not exist but because it has not yet been proven or labeled—that created the universe, then you can start to understand the information in this book.

Determine the Outcome of Your Life

I wanted to recreate my life-changing experience to show you how it applies to the issue of "how life works." I will spend my life explaining it because, even though the explanations may seem basic in the simple sense, the answer remains complicated to implement. If I have expounded my thoughts appropriately, you may have found some of my insights personally helpful to enhance the way you live your life with some incredibly uplifting results. It all makes sense if you just allow yourself to be open to new thoughts.

If you've read this book with an open mind, a mindset full of possibility, and an intellectual thirst for the truth, it's possible that you've found your own tools to enable you to start to understand how life works. YOU and only YOU can make it happen!

With "The Power of Knowing How Life Works", you can now start changing the world. I hope this book helps you sort out some of your "why" questions and gave you simple answers that you can use.

"The Knowledge", which I have manifested, is critical information. If you care about your future, your family's future, and humanities future—and eventually the future of the world—you need to absorb it.

My ego is not speaking when I say things like; "The Knowledge" will change the world. The insights were truly that powerful. Whether or not you have accepted its potential, I must continue to move in that direction.

You will say I have a choice! I do not; "The Knowledge" is just too powerful to ignore!

Where's Your Focus?

I have asked many people, "What did you want to do with your life when you were younger?" The majority said that they had no specific goals or objectives; they just wanted to be happy and comfortable. Some mentioned that they wanted a family; others said that they were "hoping" for good health, a great job, and a nice car—hoping that destiny would be good to them. Many had a fantasy wish about being a movie star or a professional athlete, but they never focused enough on these dreams to make them realities. Some felt as if they had too many options, some felt they had none.

I am always perplexed that so many people do not have a specific focus about how they want their lives to turn out—or, at the very least, a tiny bit of curiosity as to how it all works! Some just exist and think that life works based on chance or destiny. These people eventually find themselves in a place and they don't understand how or why they got there!

When depression and pressure set in, which are typical symptoms of this confusion, it is necessary to ask a few tough questions:

- Do I blame my environment?
- Was it up to me?
- Did I just miss it?

Ask your friends whether they planned their lives. Did they end up doing what they are doing by chance? Did they just take life as it came along?

For the most part, society has taught us that the definition of "how life works" is to wake up in the morning, go to work and earn some money to pay the bills, then start all over the next day. If you live this way, you are not alone. The majority of the world lives their lives in a very similar fashion. In fact, some people have found it much easier to sit back, wait for the government check to arrive, and rely on someone else to control their lives. They know they do not feel good about doing that, but it is an easy way out and they take it. Get up, take action, manifest some powerful knowledge and move forward.

Other people—perhaps even you—may be encouraged by another's strength and positive attitudes. At times though, you may find yourself drawn into life's negative feelings. Perhaps you feel hopeless about the direction your life has taken or the path you've chosen. You might even be contemplating a reason not to live.

We are just ordinary people, but if you are in neutral hoping that it all works out; surviving because of other people's actions, environmental situations, or specific events, it becomes easy to assume that we have lost control or have ended up in situations we cannot control. Based on "The Knowledge," you would be wrong.

This may be the perfect time to look at how things are working in your life, and to take control of what might currently seem like a desperate situation and turn it into a positive—and possibly an exciting—future.

Missed Opportunities

The universe provides the options, but you alone make every decision for the type of particles you choose to attract. You cannot blame your environment—or others—for missed opportunities. Your bosses, neighbors, family, children—even your significant other—can't "fix" your life for you. Nobody can give you the life you want; *except you*. Even if someone handed you a million dollars, it would still be up to you to weigh the options to take it or not based on the consequences.

It's Up to You

You can control your life and the environment in which you live, and almost every situation that you face, by understanding and accepting "The Power of Knowing How Life Works". For example, if you want to feel positive every day, "The Knowledge" will show you how to think positive thoughts, feel positive feelings, and set your surroundings to support these choices. You can have a tremendously healthy, happy, and prosperous life, regardless of your age, weight, or marital status—*and it's up to you!*

I will not tell you how to make the changes in order to live a fulfilled and happy life, nor will I help you decide which fork in the road to take as you travel the path of your life. I cannot be your personal advocate nor can I outline a direct path for you. *You have to empower yourself.*

I wrote this book to remind you to make that personal, simple decision. I also wrote it to show you how you can go from the lowest point in your life (as I did) to a significant and prosperous life.

"Sure, Don, we *get* it. We have heard it all before. It would be great if we *could* feel positive every day and walk around with a smile and a euphoric feeling of joy, but *how do we do that?*"

You do it by carefully listening to and developing "The Knowledge", provided to you through "The Power of Knowing How Life Works". By simply utilizing positive instead of negative energy in your life, you can dramatically change your life for the better.

When you understand "The Power of Knowing How Life Works," you will be able to implement the changes you want for yourself; *because you want to*—and you believe you can; not because of the words I am writing in this book.

Spreading "The Knowledge"

When I asked myself the question, "How is it working so far?" I received an overwhelmingly powerful insight: I am supposed to focus on and distribute "The Knowledge" to people who are not aware of the kinds of principles about which I speak. While those who attend seminars or are in support groups often have a much better foundation to accept "The Knowledge," they are not the people who need it; they are the people who will help distribute it.

You may be a member of a small group of the world's population who already "gets it." Perhaps you have a good handle on how life should work. You may come from a religious, spiritual, or scientific community, or have a holistic background, which contributes to feeling more positive every day.

Although "The Knowledge" is an affirmation for all of us, I am aware that it was not provided to me in an attempt to change who you are. Rather, if you are a person who "gets it," perhaps this material will move you to want to share it with others.

You might even be one of the many people who are "supposed" to help me distribute "The Knowledge" to the people who "don't get it," such as skeptics, or those who appear to be uninterested or are willing to just let the proverbial chips fall where they may.

Many people are wedded to their religious or political beliefs to the point of wearing blinders; others have given up on religion because they didn't find the answers they were searching for or have endured a loss that has taken them off course. Some are heavily influenced by their environment, politics, religion, or prejudice, who are being pulled along a path that is beneficial to them but that also supports a particular person or leader's ego-based agenda.

Passing Through the Information Line

Have you ever played the game called "Telephone," where you whispered information from person to person down a line, and the person at the end of the line said something very different from what was originally spoken by the first person?

My information came directly from the source, which by now you understand is the universal knowledge base. I know that fact without hesitation based on the insights that arrived with it. Just as the Christian couple that walked in my store continued to explain to me that they received their information "indirectly" from the source, I have learned to listen and not confront traditional beliefs. My challenge during these discussions is that people explain their deep beliefs but cannot tell me that they spoke directly to their source. They have learned and accepted their beliefs through the proverbial information line. It really does not matter as long as the path they are on rewards them with positive results. The ironic thing that I am well aware of is that by receiving "The Knowledge" through me you are still not getting it directly from the source but I am a powerful link for you.

Regardless of what information you have, please confirm that it comes directly from the source or at least as close as you can get for now and its meaning has not been lost in translation. My insights confirm that the universe wants you to read these words written from the source—the pure source. If you believe you are, then you are drawing positive energy from your belief and I support your belief as pure. If you are not in direct contact with the source, take time to closely evaluate all of "The Knowledge" and then make your own decisions. I encourage you to do so even with "The Knowledge" that I am passing along to you. The reason that I have the confidence to say that is the fact that my knowledge comes from a source that you can also tap into. The universal data base; which source created the data base is up to you to determine.

Many people believe they already get it. Somehow, we have to take it outside that small circle of people and get it to the world. People are losing their jobs, their homes, their families, and their lives to suicide. We still have war, divorce, gangs, homelessness, depression, crime, drugs, and alcohol abuse. The list goes on.

It is up to you and only you. The phenomenon works because, even though the explanations of "how life works" may seem basic in the simple explanation, the answer to that nagging question remains complicated to implement.

How is it working so far?

It's *not*—at least for the majority of people who have at least one aspect of their lives that routinely knocks them off course. In fact, it seems that, when you get one thing fixed in your life, something else pops up (for example, lack of self-esteem, love, friendships, education, or work) and the cycle continues.

A complete feeling of security surrounds me now. I have gained a new understanding of the high potential for peace and prosperity in the world through self-reflection, which I know can exist because I have seen it clearly. I no longer am ready for retirement. I have a huge job to do!

I now work for you.

What It All Means to You

I have decided to end this book with a summary of what it all means to *you,* the reader. I want you to understand that you do not have to be a scholar, philosopher, PhD, theologian, or Harvard graduate to understand this information. I am "just an ordinary guy" just like you, except that, one morning, I woke up to an amazing experience, which has changed my life.

I can only hope that I can help you, in some small way, change your life (if you need change); if not, keep doing what you are doing. I have plenty of other potential people awaiting "The Knowledge".

If your life is great, you have total confidence in your future, and you have always felt empowered to help others but did not know how, *this is the time to help me change the world.* I need you. Soon, you will know how you can help. Prepare for feeling good about your accomplishments by being able to give back to those people who have not yet figured it all out. The "Shift" that we see in the economic world, the personal turmoil, the change in attitudes both good and bad are real. They are caused by our thoughts!

On the surface, "The Knowledge" that came my way may seem basic. Many of you will say that it has been delivered before in many forms.

Well, here's one last attempt: *How is it working so far?*

So, if you do not believe that the experience happened, I do not take it personally. I will assume that you may or may not understand, and will do my best to be a good steward of

"The Knowledge". I will be impeccable with my word going forward in order to gain your trust and confidence.

Many others have tried to relate "The Knowledge," but few are trained to distribute it or have not recognized their training and therefore discounted it. There will be checkpoints that only they will possess. Earthly time will bring us together and measure our progress, we will know if the other person has received "The Knowledge" from the original source: "the universe." or if they are pretending.

It is highly possible that others have received "The Knowledge" in the same manner; only earthly time will let us all know that answer. I am actually very interested in knowing if others have received "The Knowledge" and am extremely interested if it arrived around the same time. Society may have locked them up already and thrown away the key.

"The Knowledge" can exist among other existing belief systems:

- The scientific community need not discount "The Knowledge" as it was not sent to discredit science in any way but rather to encourage further investigation into things like the zero-point field and beyond. Water plays a critical role in the scientific understanding of how it all works.

- Research scientists should not give up cell research or any research relating to the cure of cancer or other diseases. However, the area that surrounds the cell allows for communication between the cells. The phenomenon can either be the catalyst that spreads disease or the mode to block the communication. (Researchers: Keep up your important work, but look outside the cell.)

- The religious community need not be concerned because "The Knowledge" is universal to all beliefs; in fact, you can apply your spiritual, personal, or scientific thoughts without the fear that usually emanates from unsubstantiated information. Particles of thought could have been placed by anyone, including a superior being.

This is not a personal belief or scientific theory. It is also not my personal guess or theory. It is pure knowledge waiting to be investigated. Others will need to focus on the science behind it.

The investigation will be easier in this century because people are more receptive to new ideas and thoughts about how life began and how it continues. Think about how long the old myths have lasted, and how ready we are for the truth of how it all really works. "The Knowledge" provides a different place to look for answers that traditional thinking humans may have overlooked.

If you already know certain facts, let's talk; however, first ask yourself this question: "How is the fact that you understand, that single component of the big picture working so far?" It's like the research around the zero-point fields. It's interesting stuff, but do we know how it applies to how life works? Now we do!

Use Your Power to Change the World

It does not take a Harvard scholar to determine that the world is in crisis. America is in crisis. The American workforce is in crisis. Our companies, communities, schools, educational systems, and families are in crisis. However, globally, we are seeing a shift of thought. More people are searching for answers because, when they ask themselves the question, "How is it working so far?" they conclude, "It is not!"

They no longer accept influences from their environment. They want to make their own decisions and draw their own conclusions. "The Power of Knowing How Life Works" is a necessary tool in this process. For example; the surge of uprisings in the Middle East are a direct result of the masses utilizing "The Power of Knowing How Life Works" without even knowing that they, as a group are using it. Let me explain; because of the power of thought that exist in the universe it is possible for people to share beliefs, feelings and thoughts readily through the communications allowed via the phenomenon that exist. When a large group of people start to believe that they have had enough of a particular dictator they band together and create change. Now many times that change involves violence but more and more we are seeing that the masses can implement change without violence simply by sharing the same common goals and yes, thoughts.

They come from a neutral state into a state of manifesting change and it works because of "The Power of Knowing How Life Works". The bad guys no longer will have control and if we all focus on peace instead of violence it will be manifested. The powerful thoughts that surround us all, will create a change in the phenomenon and a shift in the conscious movement in the universe and will supply the shift that will take place.

How is "it"—your life, your circumstances, your negativity, politics, or the collective religions of the world—working so far? If your answer is also, "It is not," please keep reading my books. In fact, keep reading even if you embrace the concept of positive thinking and are getting from life every wonderful thing you believe life has to offer. You can help me share "The Knowledge" with the world and make a difference.

To "empower" means to "give someone the authority or power to do something; enable someone to do something; make someone stronger and more confident, especially in controlling their life and claiming their path forward." The universe—or some other source, depending on your beliefs—has empowered me to empower you to have a happier life and improve the world picture.

Since our energy dissipates after we die, and reconnects with others based on our mutual levels of attraction in many different ways and over many different people's lives, we are all connected. Whether you are out in the woods wearing camouflage and hunting, standing in an unemployment line, or walking through downtown San Francisco with a briefcase full of progressive ideas, you have access to "The Knowledge" and can utilize it.

Can you imagine the shift that might occur if everyone understood *how* we are connected? What might happen if everyone understood the *depth* of our mutual connection and that we truly are a part of each other? What if people really understood the *power* of their thoughts and how all this works? Just imagine how different the world might become if the seven billion people on our planet could live better, more powerful lives by just realizing that all of humanity is united as one. Then we create the shift that makes it a reality simply by everyone thinking peace and harmony.

As you learn how to become a leader of positive change in your life, take charge of your thoughts, and develop your own empowerment, you will reap many benefits. If you help spread "The Knowledge"—regardless of race, creed, religious belief, sexual orientation, gender, or any other condition—we can empower others to change the world and make it a happier, better, and safer place to live.

You have power. Use that power to change the world. For example, if you are a constant skeptic of new ideas, consider thinking "out of the box." If you produce tabloids that exploit evil rather than create good for the world, change your approach and instead report on the teacher who spends her own money on school supplies instead of the junkie who robs the 7-Eleven or the movie star that got drunk and disorderly. Stop the madness!

Let's work together in thought and make a difference—*a big difference*. The good news is that it is already working with no explanation. *Now we know why!*

By understanding "The Power of Knowing How Life Works," and accepting how the energy around you works, you will make a difference and enjoy your life. Embrace "The Knowledge" with your families and in your schools, communities, and neighborhoods. Make the shift one or two individuals at a time.

We must teach our youth before they get to the point in their lives where violence is the assumed cure-all. However, it may take a few future generations for them to understand the missing ingredient: "The Knowledge", complete with insights, providing "The Power of Knowing How Life Works".

Traditional values have indoctrinated current generations. As humanity evolves with the new consciousness provided by the universe, it will be easier for future generations to adapt to the changes in philosophy. Perhaps a future generation will start to explore, pursue, and attract the scientific analysis of the phenomenon to the necessary depth. Imagine being able to see thoughts, feelings, beliefs, knowledge and information. It all resides in a yet undiscovered dimension. It is real and it is spectacular.

Get involved.

Enjoy Your Life Along The Way

Now that you know where "The Knowledge" comes from, it is up to you to utilize it appropriately. You must imagine, ask, attract, and be patient without false expectations.

For example, my entire life was good. Without knowing technically that I was manifesting a good life, I was doing just that: *manifesting.* I can look at every step of my life and confirm that I used the process of manifestation to get where I am today, which is sharing "The Knowledge" with you.

Here's another example: When I wanted to transfer from one sales territory to another, I would manifest the move and declare my work in that geographic location complete, ready for a new challenge in some other location. Soon, through my tenacity and of course now I know my manifesting ability, I was offered a corporate move. I moved six times and the company paid for the buying and selling of my personal residence and the cost of relocating, which was quite unusual, and very expensive. Once moved, if I wanted a certain type of house, I would manifest the type and general location of the community in which I wanted to live. I did not get specific during the process, and never identified that what I was doing was manifesting. I just imagined, asked, believed, and accepted the results that I attracted. Looking back, it really was quite remarkable.

If you are struggling with this aspect of "The Knowledge," trace the steps through your life. As you start to believe that it is exactly how your life unfolded, you will also start to accept that "The Knowledge" is pure.

Don't discount your manifestation as not working because of man-made timeframes. Enjoy your life along the way, and believe that you have "The Power of Knowing How Life Works". The universe will deliver answers to you in some form in some earthly time slot. When that happens, be ready to accept the answers when they arrive. Remember; reduce your frustration concerning time; as there is no "time" in the universe.

Many people do not recognize the answers or discount their arrival, and then miss the very same opportunity for which they have been asking. For example, someone who wants to be a dancer is introduced to a dance instructor at a party. This person says nice things and then leaves. Always take advantage of each introduction. It could lay out the path for your future. Look at each individual not with judgment or prejudice but rather that they are "The Knowledge" being delivered for you at that point in earthly time.

Do not stop living your life by waiting for good things to happen. Create them using "The Power of Knowing How Life Works"!

The People in My Life

Before Nov. 17, 2009, I would have ignored many of the people who came into my life. I now realize that if they came into my life, they are there for a purpose or a reason, and I give them special attention. Either I need them or they need me, but they are no longer just an occurrence nor do I take their arrival into my life for granted. Keep in mind that it really does not matter who did the attracting. The important piece is that you acknowledge their physical and spiritual presence.

I believe that others may not have recognized "The Knowledge" as real or haven't been open to receiving the insights that followed it. Others may have received their insights and answers by way of the Law of Attraction, manifestation, intuition, spiritual awareness, prayer or some other means. However, I do believe that, if I do not share "The Knowledge", it will be taken from me in some way and will be lost back into the universe until someone else manifests it again. I have a big responsibility but I am proud to accept it.

If you have heard it all before—the "think positively" inspirational and motivational mumbo jumbo—you have a right to be skeptical. Why should you listen to me? I realize (just as you are now realizing) that we have no choice but to get better.

Our future—and our children's future—depend on it.

Does One of These Faces Belong to You?

During my November 2009 experience, images of many people ran through my thoughts like a 3D movie. As they walk into my life now, I immediately recognize their presence, even if I cannot match their face with the movie that ran through my mind. I know that these people hold some future significance in my life as I keep learning about how to distribute "The Knowledge".

When I am in a crowded room, I often sense the presence of at least one of these people, but I do not know who they are. I now embrace the feeling instead of feeling confused by it. When this happens, I introduce myself and, before long, the person will say something like, "Oh, Aunt Sally is a publisher,"

"I am a producer for NBC," or "My dad is in radio." It is amazing how the universe provides the people I need; however, it works both ways. Some are money-motivated, some are curious, and some truly understand the need to get "The Knowledge" distributed.

This last type of person—one who truly understands the need to get "The Knowledge" distributed—will listen, focus, care about, and offer to distribute "The Knowledge" and help the world along the way. They do not have a "what's in for me" attitude. They come to the surface like oil on water and often become part of my core team.

I am well on my way to finding them. They feel the energy but have not yet been provided with "The Power of Knowing How Life Works". They will eventually receive it and we will have a powerful team to distribute "The Knowledge". They will know—not because I will have chosen them, but because the universe has chosen us.

This is not about destiny. People manifest the path to take them where they want to go by accessing the powerful knowledge already in the universe. My core team will have manifested and thus attracted the path to help change the world for the better. We will be joined by hundreds even thousands along the way that will utilize "The Knowledge" to convert their passion for a better world into real-life actions, and then apply those actions to the transformation of a conscious, abundant, and empowering life for everyone.

The Box (Again)

Your thoughts and beliefs, which you have stored safely in the box, belong to you; "The Knowledge", which I received on Tuesday, Nov. 17, 2009, at 6:24 a.m., also belongs to you. I am merely the vehicle that the universe is using to deliver it. You remain in complete control.

Now that you have read this book, please do the following exercise:

1. Open the box.
2. You will find your traditional values, religious teachings and beliefs, political beliefs, and any prejudices you may have accumulated exactly where they were when you started reading this book.
3. If you feel that I've taken you places you did not wish to go, take back whatever values or traditional thoughts you want or need.
4. However, I personally would like to see you leave your old baggage and issues, and most importantly, your PREJUDICE, in the box forever and close the lid. This would be a good start.

Only you can determine what you would like to accept and what you would like to leave in the box. As you have discovered, everything goes back into the universe for someone else to utilize. It's how it works.

This book is not the end of the discussion. It is the beginning of our amazing journey together.

Let us begin!

Meditation Moment:

Close your eyes if you wish and imagine that you are surrounded by small dots and waves. You are in tune with the universe, nothing else matters right at this moment accept your awareness with the fact you are sitting in the middle of all of these dots and waves and they surround you as if you are sitting suspended in midair.

The dots have a unique characteristic about them they can pass right through you; focus on one dot as it starts on your right side, passes through you and ends up on your left side and waves are continuous and pass through from one side to the other of your body as if you are transparent. You can keep the dot on your left near you or let it keep going; dispersing the dot back into the universe.

You have control over whether to let the dot pass through you or whether to stop it "within" you; maybe you just let it stay with other dots that surround you so you can process it through your body at a later time. Imagine that 50 trillion of your cells are made up of water, and the water has memory and can communicate with the dots, your mind, your heart, your entire body is communicating with the dots and waves fueled by the water that makes up 85% of your biological existence.

Let's sit quietly as we enjoy the dots and waves, some of them we would like to keep; others make us feel bad and we want them to leave; some are filled with love and hope; some are confusing us filled with mixed emotions and thoughts.

Remember You and only You have total control; YOU AND ONLY YOU ! Get to choose which ones you keep and which ones pass on into the universe.

The dots are the particles of thoughts, feelings, beliefs, emotions and knowledge that are creating our reality; your reality in turn creates humanities reality and the combined thoughts create the universal reality that controls our world.

You are sitting in the middle of Universal consciousness or if you prefer a universal computer; the collective mind; you feel good because finally, you are in control of YOU! You possess The Power of Knowing How Life Works... "The Knowledge"

Bibliography

Assaraf, John and Murray Smith. *The Answer: Grow Any Business, Achieve Financial Freedom, and Live an Extraordinary Life* (Atria, 2008).

Byrne, Rhonda. *The Secret* (Atria Books/Beyond Words, 2006).
"The Francis Crick Papers: The Discovery of the Double Helix, 1951-1953 (http://profiles.nlm.nih.gov/SC); "The Discovery of the Molecular Structure of DNA—The Double Helix" (http://nobelprize.org/educational/medicine/dna_double_helix/readmore.html).

"The Four Agreements" from Toltec Spirit: Commence Sense Wisdom for the Spiritual Warrior's Journey (www.toltecspirit.com).

Selby, John, et al. *Tapping the Source: Using the Master Key System for Abundance and Happiness* (Sterling Ethos, 2010).

Testimonials:

"When I learned about the information Don had been given, I was curious. In a time when so many people seem to have the next 'new, in the know' information, I wondered what he could know that was so unique. What I learned was that Don had been truly blessed with deep insights that will affect millions of people. If you want to live from your most powerful self, you will want to know Don's information."

— Katy Stanley ~ Founder, The Goddessey Institute

"I hear a lot of people speak about spirituality from all walks of life. I appreciate Don's insights because they are so universal. They are a vehicle for spiritual oneness."

— David Stanley ~ Author of Conversations With The King

"This book is a major game changer for our understanding about how the universe works. I was blown away by the Knowledge. Don gave me a whole new way of looking at my existence. If you get excited about being on the cutting edge of consciousness, this is it."

— Randy Peyser, author of "The Power of Miracle Thinking", www.authoronestop.com

"Every once in a while, the Universe / God / Source, taps someone on the forehead and says "Here is the Truth – go share it". The world is then blessed with another expression of Divine

Consciousness and we are all enlightened by the message. My friend Don has been a true and faithful steward to his gift, and in his sharing, brings a beautiful light to everyone. I am inspired, and I know that you will be, too."

— Paul Hoyt, author of "The Practice of Awakening"
www.capitalcoachingprogram.com

"A must read for seekers of the "real" knowledge of how life works for each earthly being --before, during, and after the physical existence. You won't be disappointed"

- Sandra Weber, Retired Businesswoman, Hospice volunteer,
Long-time Cancer survivor

"**WOW** what a powerful **MESSAGE;** couldn't put it down can't **WAIT** for the next book"

-Aimmee Kodachian, Author of Tears of
Hope www.empoweringsoulsint.com

"Don's message will lighten your stress going forward and bring perfect balance into your life right now. Before you know it you will begin to experience a perspective over your precious life at a very high level."

— David L. Haman, Managing Partner
at Valley Green Financial

I worked with Don during multiple business transactions, awesome guy. Completely trustworthy, always giving; helping mankind one person at a time. Don's book will help you to become self-reliant so that in turn you can be prepared to help others.

- Neil Dabney, CEO, Dabney and Associates.

I manifested the meeting with Don as I have been looking for my own answers. From the first moment I sat with him to learn of "The Knowledge" I am convinced he was given the answers, the information, and the guidance that our world is so desperately in need of, not only to regain its balance, but to function with the beautiful existence it is capable of. Don was given "The Knowledge" many of us have been searching for.

- Missy Bystrom, CEO " The Organized Connection"
missy@theorganizedconnection.com

Printed in the United States
by Baker & Taylor Publisher Services